540 7

35.64

D1529301

Experimenting with
Chemistry

 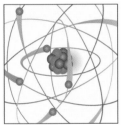  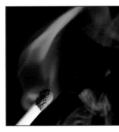  

John Farndon

Marshall Cavendish
Benchmark

Marshall Cavendish Benchmark
99 White Plains Road
Tarrytown, New York 10591
www.marshallcavendish.us

Library of Congress Cataloging-in-Publication Data

Farndon, John.
  Experimenting with chemistry / by John Farndon. – 1st ed.
      p. cm. – (Experimenting with science)
  Summary: "Explores and explains chemistry concepts and provides experiments to aid in understanding chemistry"–Provided by publisher.
  Includes index.
  ISBN 978-0-7614-3928-8
  1. Chemistry–Experiments–Juvenile literature. I. Title.
  QD38.F374 2009
  540.78–dc22

                    2008017570

Cover design by Virginia Pope
The photographs in this book are used by permission and through the courtesy of:
Shutterstock: front cover, back cover, 1; R, 6; Kameel4u, 7; fotoadamczyk, 8; Perov Stanislav, 12; J. Helgason, 16; Nikita Tiunov, 17; Dewitt, 18; Igor Smichkov, 20; George Lee, 23; Eduardo Rivero, 26; Alan Dunlop-Walters, 27; Sebastian Kaulitzki, 30; Peter Zharov, 32; Shi Yali, 38; Kmitu, 39; Margrit, 42; Vyacheslav Osokin, 43; Jose AS Reyes, 46; Fillipp Bezlutskiy, 56; Christopher Elwell, 62; Jhaz Photography, 72; RCPPHOTO, 76; Mike Flippo, 82; 4uphoto.pt, 90; ? 94; iofoto, 96; 3445128471, 97. **Marshall Cavendish:** 34, 52, 66, 68; photographs by Martin Norris, 10, 11, 14, 15, 18, 19, 20, 22, 23, 24, 25, 28, 29, 36, 37, 40, 41, 44, 45, 48, 49, 50, 51, 53, 54, 55, 57, 58, 59, 60, 61, 63, 64, 65, 69, 70, 71, 73, 74, 75, 77, 78, 79, 80, 81, 83, 84, 85, 86, 87, 88, 89, 92, 93, 94, 95, 98, 99.

Printed in Malaysia

1 2 3 4 5 6

Contents

What Is Chemistry?

What are things made of? How do substances combine to form new substances? Chemistry helps to explain the answers to these questions. At a basic level, chemistry is the study of substances—or matter—and their properties. This branch of science explores concepts, such as what matter is made of, how it behaves, and how it interacts with other substances.

All matter is made from combinations of substances called elements. Elements are made up of tiny atoms. These atoms are too small to see, but are the basic building blocks of all matter. Atoms of different elements have different properties and behave in various ways.

What happens when you mix two substances together? In most cases, their atoms interact and a chemical reaction occurs. The mixture might fizzle, turn another color, or even start to smell. Parts of the mixture might even evaporate, or turn to gas. When combined in the right amounts, common household substances like vinegar and baking soda will yield a chemical reaction that is easy to see.

Not all changes involve chemical reactions. You know that an ice cube is just a block of frozen water. Frozen or liquid, water might take different shapes or take up different amounts of space, or volume, but it is still water. Changing states—from solid to liquid to gas—does not affect water's chemical makeup. Simple experiments with ice cubes and water can show these types of scientific principles.

The science experiments in this book will help you understand these kinds of chemistry concepts—and many more. Through careful thought and a little experimentation, you can see and understand how chemistry affects you in every way.

Colorful fireworks are an example of chemical reactions at work. Different elements — including magnesium, barium, and sodium — combine with heat and other substances to create these bright displays.

Chemicals

The word "chemicals" makes people think of laboratories full of steaming jars and dangerous liquids. In fact, chemicals are not just weird substances that scientists play with. Every substance on Earth and in the whole universe is made from chemicals, from plain tap water to exotic metals deep underground. Indeed, your body and every other living thing is made entirely of chemicals. Even the air around us is made from a combination of chemicals.

Just as a cake is made up from different ingredients, everything is made from combinations of chemicals. Some substances, like table salt, are made up of just one main chemical, while others, like human skin, are made from many. The same chemicals can be found in many different substances. It is the special combination of chemicals that makes each substance the way it is.

Most chemicals are everyday substances. Only a few are strange-looking fluids in laboratory flasks like these.

Did you know?

The foundations of the science of chemistry were laid by the alchemists of the Middle Ages. The alchemists brewed and mixed substances in the vain hope of finding a magical substance that would turn iron to gold. Many of the first great alchemists were Arab, and the word *alchemy* comes from the Arabic *al quemia*, which is said to mean the art of pouring.

PHYSICAL PROPERTIES

These are some of the physical properties that chemicals can have:

- State: Is it a solid, a liquid, or a gas? At what temperature does it boil, freeze, or melt?
- Appearance: What color is it? Is it shiny or dull? Is it clear or opaque?
- Texture and shape: Is it a powder or a crystal? Is it rough or smooth to the touch? Is it oily or watery?
- Plasticity: Does it bend, stretch, or squash easily?
- Elasticity: Does it spring back to its original shape after bending, stretching, or squashing?
- Toughness: How hard is it? Does it break easily?
- Density: How heavy is it?
- Buoyancy: Does it float?
- Heat properties: Is it cold to the touch? Does it heat up or cool down quickly?

Glass is easy to identify by its physical properties. It is hard and clear, but also very brittle and shatters easily.

Each chemical has its own properties and a scientific name. Salt, for example, is made of the chemical called sodium chloride. Some properties are simply physical—what the chemical looks like, how it feels to the touch, how it reacts to being bent, hit, pulled, and so on. "Chemical" properties are how a chemical reacts with another chemical. Baking powder and talcum powder are both fine, white powders, so are physically similar. Yet they are chemically different because baking powder reacts with vinegar to create a froth; talcum powder does not react at all.

ELEMENTS AND COMPOUNDS

Gold is highly resistant to corrosion, which is why it nearly always shines. This is also why it is one of the very few elements to occur naturally in pure form. Gold atoms have 79 protons each.

There are billions of different substances in the universe. Yet, remarkably, all these different substances are made from few more than 100 basic chemicals called elements. Iron, oxygen, and hydrogen are all examples of elements.

Every substance can be broken down into increasingly simple chemicals until it is separated into the elements it is made from. Elements are the simplest possible substances, and cannot normally be broken down any further. It takes extreme conditions like the incredibly hot core of a star to break elements down.

Ninety-two elements are known to occur naturally. But scientists have created more than thirty in the laboratory, such as the strangely named ununhexium and ununoctium, and also seaborgium, named after scientist Glenn Seaborg. Many of these laboratory-created elements sometimes flash into existence for no more than a fraction of a second.

Some substances, such as gold, are made from just one element. If they occur naturally, they are called native elements. Others that contain two or more elements joined together are called compounds. Table salt, for example, is a compound of two elements, sodium and chlorine, which is

ATOMS

Every element and compound—and so every substance in the universe— is made up from incredibly tiny particles called atoms. Atoms are so small, two billion would fit on the period at the end of this sentence. Atoms are mostly empty space dotted with even tinier particles. In the center is the nucleus or core, made from two kinds of particle—protons and neutrons. Around the nucleus are the smallest particles of all, electrons. Each atom usually has an equal number of protons and electrons, and the way an atom behaves depends on just how many there are. Each of the different elements is made from atoms with a certain number of protons. Hydrogen atoms are the smallest of all atoms, with just a single proton. Iron atoms have 26 protons. Uranium atoms have 92, the most that occur naturally in an atom.

Electrons orbiting in layers

Nucleus with protons and neutrons

This is an artwork of an atom, showing the nucleus (core) with layers of electrons orbiting around it.

why it has the chemical name sodium chloride.

Surprisingly, compounds have completely different properties than the elements that make them. Sodium is actually a soft metal that burns when put in water. Chlorine is a thick, poisonous, green gas.

CHEMICALS AT HOME

You will need

✔ Household items such as bowls, bottles, spoons, and screws. Choose objects made from a single material, rather than complex objects like radios, which are made from many materials.

1 Start by separating out metals, which are often shiny, hard, and feel cold. Stone is also cold and hard but not usually shiny.

Material groups

This is one way you can group household materials, with some of the properties you can use to identify them and the chemicals they are made from.

METALS like iron and copper are:
often shiny, strong, hard, dense, bendable, conduct heat and electricity well, may react with air, water, and acids.
Chemical: Metal elements

CERAMICS like china and bricks are:
hard, strong in some directions, brittle, heat resistant, chemically unreactive.
Chemical: Silicon, oxygen, aluminium, hydrogen

PLASTICS like PVC vary but most are:
flexible, easily melted and molded, may burn when heated in air
Chemical: Carbon, hydrogen, various nonmetals

GLASSES are:
like ceramics, but transparent
Chemical: Silicon, oxygen, various metal elements

FIBERS are:
flexible, burn when heated in air, form long hair-like strands
Chemical: Carbon, hydrogen, various nonmetals

NATURAL MATERIALS such as wood and stone:
vary greatly
Chemical: Most elements (wood is carbon and hydrogen)

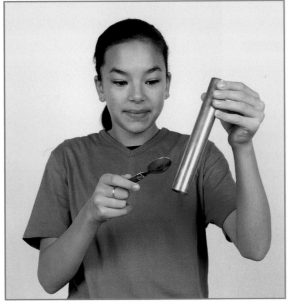

Take it further

Once you have separated out the metal objects, see if you can separate out all the other objects made from a single material and find ways of grouping them. Decide, for instance, if the material is natural, like wood, or human-made, like glass and plastics. Then try grouping the human-made materials into ceramics, plastics, glasses, and fibers. See if you can identify

2 To confirm a substance is metal, knock it gently with a spoon. Metals often make a clanging sound.

Brass

Stainless steel

Copper

Silver

Gold

Aluminum

Steel

Chromium

Iron

Of the more than 90 elements that occur naturally, 81 are metals. They are useful for making things because, although strong, they can be bent, hammered, or molded into shape. Most metals have "tensile strength," which means they can support a heavy load. This is why large structures such as buildings and bridges are often made of metal. Each metal has its own special properties. Many metals you find around the home are not elements, but combinations called alloys, which unite the properties of various metals. Brass is an alloy of copper and zinc.

Tin and other metals

CHEMICALS TOGETHER

The atoms of some elements, like helium, exist on their own. But most join up with each other. When atoms link together, they form a new particle called a molecule.

Molecules are the smallest parts of a chemical to exist alone. Some are single atoms, but most are combinations. Atoms of hydrogen, for instance, usually pair up. Hydrogen gas is really hydrogen molecules, made from pairs of atoms.

When atoms of one element join atoms of another, they form

The water we rely on for so many things is a compound of hydrogen and oxygen. In every molecule of water, two hydrogen atoms combine with one oxygen atom.

In focus

COVALENT BONDS

Nonmetal atoms have too few electrons for a full outer shell. But they can get a full set by sharing pairs with each other. The shared electrons are pulled equally by electrical attraction towards the nuclei of each atom, so the atoms bind together with their electron shells overlapping. Electron-sharing bonds like this are called covalent. A carbon atom can bond like this with four atoms at once, which is why it can make many compounds.

Shared electrons

IONIC BONDS

Most metal atoms have just one or two electrons in their outer shell. They can get a full shell by giving these "spares" away. Many nonmetal atoms have too few electrons, so readily capture the metal's spares. Electrons have a negative electrical charge. Losing them gives the metal atom a positive charge; gaining them gives the nonmetal a negative charge. The two oppositely charged atoms are drawn together by electrical attraction, like opposite magnetic poles. Charged atoms are called ions, so this is an ionic bond. Unlike covalent bonds, the attraction is between whole atoms, not just electrons.

Sodium atom gives up an electron

Chlorine atom gains an electron

Mutual electrical attraction

Electrons in their shells

Sodium atoms have one "spare" electron; chlorine atoms have one "missing." So when they meet, the sodium atom donates an electron to the chlorine. The atoms bond to make a molecule of sodium chloride (table salt) by mutual electrical attraction.

a compound. Compounds are never individual atoms, but identical molecules.

Some molecules are simple. Water is one atom of oxygen and two of hydrogen. Others are much bigger. Plastics have giant molecules, built from long chains of atoms.

An atom's readiness to link up to form molecules—and its whole chemical behavior—depends on its electron set-up. An atom's electrons sit in onion-like layers or "shells." For reasons scientists only barely understand, an atom likes to have a "full" outer shell, with the right number of electrons.

Atoms like helium that do have full shells are chemically slow to react and rarely form molecules. But most atoms have too many or too few electrons and readily form molecules. When they meet other atoms, they lose, capture, or share electrons to get a full set—that is, they react chemically. It is these interactions that bind atoms into molecules.

There are two main kinds of bond: ionic and covalent. When different atoms meet and bond, they form a compound. But different atoms can meet and not interact. This is called a mixture.

MIXTURES

You will need

- ✔ Four small jars
- ✔ Four small dishes for mixing
- ✔ Food coloring and ink
- ✔ Paper strips
- ✔ An eye dropper
- ✔ Clips and pencils to hold the strips in place

1 Pour small quantities of different food color and inks into each dish to make four different mixtures of colors.

In focus

A mixture of sand and iron powder can be separated by using a magnet to draw out the iron.

MIXTURES

A few everyday substances are made of just one chemical element or compound, such as table salt (sodium chloride). But most are mixtures of several. Food, gasoline, and even air are mixtures. The various chemicals in a mixture may be so thoroughly mixed that it looks like one substance. But they do not react together and, like different marbles in a bag, their molecules remain intact. This means the properties of a mixture are really a combination of those of the different ingredients. So a mix of sugar and water is both sweet and wet. Also, with the right technique, the chemicals in a mixture can be separated out. The chromatography in the experiment is just one of many techniques for separating mixtures.

2 Using a dropper, put a tiny drop of each mixture on the end of each strip of paper.

What is happening?

As the water soaks up through the paper, it carries with it the dyes in the ink and food color. Some dyes don't dissolve well, so are left on the bottom of the paper. Others dissolve better and are carried farther up. So each dye is left at a different level. This technique for splitting colors is called "chromatography." Forensic scientists use a similar technique to help identify inks and dyes at a crime scene. Hospitals also use it to find if there is sugar in a patient's urine, which would show if he or she had diabetes. Paper is most commonly used for chromatography, but other absorbent material such as chalk can also be used.

Pour a small amount of water in each jar, then suspend each strip of paper from clips on pencils. Make sure the color drop just dips into the water. Leave for 10 minutes, and you should see how the water carries the ink up through the paper and separates it into the different colors.

CHEMICAL REACTIONS

Colorful fireworks displays are chemical reactions.

Whenever a fire burns, bread rises in an oven, or a nail becomes rusty, a chemical reaction is taking place. In the fire, the chemicals are reacting very quickly. With the nail rusting, they are reacting slowly. But each process involves elements and compounds reacting with each other, and changing in some way.

Chemical reactions are taking place everywhere all the time. All life processes depend on chemical reactions. So too do many household and industrial

Did you know?

Heat can provide the energy to speed up chemical reactions. Cooking food speeds up reactions that make food edible or tasty. Putting food in a freezer slows down the reactions that make it spoil.

processes, from the hardening of cement to the creation of new plastics.

There are many kinds of chemical reactions. Some involve just two elements or compounds reacting with each other. Others involve many more. But whenever there is a reaction, at least one of the chemicals is changed, often irreversibly, and new compounds are formed. Some bonds holding molecules together are broken and some new ones are forged.

In the real world

LIFE PROCESSES

As this dog grows, every new bit of its body will be created by chemical reactions inside each body cell.

All life depends on chemical reactions. Indeed, it might be true to say that much of life is chemical reactions. Part of the process of food digestion, for example, is a reaction between the chemicals the food is made of and body chemicals such as stomach acid. In fact, every movement of the body involves a chemical reaction, since muscles get their energy from the reaction of sugars with oxygen inside muscle cells. Plants grow because of a series of chemical reactions stimulated by sunlight in photosynthesis. In this, carbon dioxide from the air is joined to hydrogen from water to make the sugars plants use for food.

When substances just mix, they remain intact and can be separated, but when chemicals react, they really change. In fact, the formation of a new compound or the separation of a compound into its separate elements proves a reaction has taken place. Scientists usually call the original chemicals the "reactants" and the new ones formed the "products."

SIMPLE REACTIONS

You will need

- ✔ A large glass container
- ✔ A glass bowl
- ✔ Baking soda
- ✔ A couple of seltzer tablets
- ✔ A spoon
- ✔ Vinegar
- ✔ Water

1 Pour a little vinegar into a bowl—about half a cup.

In the real world

Bread rises as it is baked in the oven because it is full of expanding bubbles of carbon dioxide gas.

RAISING BREAD

One way to make bread rise and become light and fluffy is to add yeast to the dough. Yeast turns sugar in the bread to bubbles of carbon dioxide gas, making the bread swell. Another is to add baking soda and cream of tartar powder to the mix. Cream of tartar is an acid and reacts with the soda in the damp mixture, again creating bubbles of carbon dioxide in the same way as the vinegar in the experiment. Baking powder is soda with acid powder and cornstarch. The soda and acid are kept separate by the cornstarch when dry and only really react when wet.

2 Sprinkle a teaspoon of baking soda quickly into the vinegar and see how it instantly foams and makes a smell.

Some stomach-settling products are designed to react with water. Seltzer tablets and liver salts fizz when they come into contact with water. Try dipping a seltzer tablet slowly into a jar of water and watch what happens. See if you can spot how some bits sink to the bottom as the tablet dissolves. Look, too, for the gas bubbles produced as each grain hits the water. The grains make the water fizz. The green in the water here is food color added for effect.

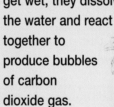

What is happening?

In the experiments with vinegar and the seltzer tablet, the fizz is a chemical reaction called "effervescence." In this, an acid dissolved in water reacts with a "base" (non-acid) to form tiny bubbles of gas (usually carbon dioxide). Vinegar is weak acetic acid and reacts strongly with the soda, which is a base, chemically known as sodium hydrogencarbonate. The seltzer tablet contains a basic salt such as magnesium sulfate, but also citric acid. While dry, the salts and acid in the tablet do not react, but as soon as they get wet, they dissolve in the water and react together to produce bubbles of carbon dioxide gas.

BURNING AND RUSTING

Oxygen, with nitrogen, is one of the two main gases in the air. It is also a highly reactive chemical, and a huge number of everyday processes are chemical reactions involving oxygen. Fires burning, metals rusting, and even breathing all involve oxygen reactions.

When oxygen reacts with a substance, it links up with the substance to form a new compound. The substance is said to be oxidized, and the process is called "oxidation."

When this happens, atoms of the oxidized substance always lose either electrons, the gas hydrogen, or both. So scientists say oxidation is any reaction in which atoms lose electrons or hydrogen—whether oxygen is involved or not.

Just as a substance can gain oxygen, it can also lose it. A substance losing its oxygen is said to be reduced. In fact, reduction always occurs at the same time as oxidation—when one substance gains oxygen,

In focus

If there is moisture in the air, steel quickly rusts as it is oxidized.

RUSTING

Iron and steel can quickly turn rusty if exposed to oxygen in the air. The oxygen destroys the iron by combining with it and turning it to iron oxide. But rust only really develops if there is moisture. Rust is not just iron oxide, but a special kind called "hydrated" iron oxide, which forms when iron oxide reacts with water. Once a surface starts to rust, it turns brittle, swells up, and flakes off. This exposes the surface to more air and water, and so rusting continues. The presence of impurities like salt accelerates the process.

another must give it up. Combined reduction and oxidation reactions are often known as redox reactions.

The most spectacular redox is burning, known by scientists as combustion. Burning usually involves a reaction between oxygen in the air and a fuel, which is the substance burned—whether it is coal, wood, gasoline, or even rubbish on a bonfire. But only gases combine readily with oxygen. If the fuel is solid or liquid, it must first get hot enough to vaporize—that is, change to a gas.

Each fuel has its own ignition point—the temperature at which it gives off enough gas to burn. Gasoline has a very low ignition point, and even a small spark is enough to make it burst explosively into flame. Wood has a much higher ignition point and may not catch fire even after sustained efforts with a match. Many substances won't burn at all at any temperature.

Fire is a violent chemical reaction, usually between oxygen and a fuel, that produces heat and light.

FIRE AND OXYGEN

You will need

- ✔ A large glass dish
- ✔ A small candle holder
- ✔ A pitcher
- ✔ A tall glass container
- ✔ Candles

1 Cut a candle in half and set it in a small holder in the center of a dish. Pour in plain tap water to half fill the dish.

2 With adult supervision, light the candle. Let it burn for a few minutes until the flame is steady.

3 Carefully lower the jar over the flame at a slight angle and stand it on the base of the dish. Note the water level in the jar.

Some fire extinguishers mix cooling water with carbon dioxide foam to smother a fire.

FIRE EXTINGUISHERS

Each kind of fire needs its own extinguisher, so canisters are color-coded. Red ones work by covering the fire with a spray of cooling water, since things only burn if hot enough. Black ones hold dense carbon dioxide gas which sinks over the fire and smothers it—so keeping out the air and depriving it of the oxygen it needs. Blue extinguishers blow out soda powder, which also settles over the fire and prevents air from reaching it.

If the flame is snuffed out instantly, take off the jar, relight the candle and try again after leaving it to burn down a little. The candle should burn inside the jar for several seconds, before finally sputtering out. As the flame dies out, watch the level of water suddenly rise inside the jar.

What is happening?

A candle gets the oxygen it needs to burn from the air. It burns only as long as there is enough oxygen in the jar. Once the oxygen is used up, the flame goes out and water gushes in to take the oxygen's place. Candle wax is a hydrocarbon, a compound of carbon and hydrogen. When it burns, oxygen links with the carbon to form carbon dioxide gas and with hydrogen to form water.

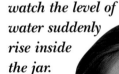

ACIDS AND BASES

All rain is slightly acidic because gases from the air, such as carbon dioxide, dissolve in raindrops as they fall. But air pollution can make the rain acidic enough to do real damage. This stone building has been damaged by acid rain.

ACIDS IN THE BODY

The human body depends on a range of acids for many processes. Hydrochloric acid in the stomach helps dissolve food, making it easier to digest. Pyruvic acid plays a vital role in converting sugar to energy in each body cell. Amino acids are the building blocks of protein, the chemicals of which the body is made. Most remarkable of all is deoxyribonucleic acid, DNA. Molecules of DNA in each body cell provide the cell's full life instructions and carry the genetic code that provides the blueprint for a new human.

The amazing spiral molecule of the acid DNA carries all the instructions for life.

Anything that tastes a little sour is probably acid. Lemon juice is citric acid. Vinegar is acetic acid. Tea contains tannic acid. Weak acids like these are found in a huge range of foods, especially fruits, and are safe to eat.

Much stronger acids, such as concentrated sulfuric and nitric acid, are used in laboratories and industry. They are very dangerous chemicals that burn clothes or skin and may even dissolve metals.

All acids, weak and strong, contain hydrogen. When they are mixed with water, the hydrogen atoms lose their one electron. Electrons have a negative electrical charge, so atoms missing an electron are positively charged and are called positive "ions."

The chemical opposite of an acid is a base. Weak bases like baking powder taste bitter or may have a soapy feel. Strong bases like caustic soda are dangerous and corrosive.

When a base reacts with an acid, it cancels out the acidity, neutralizing the acid. The acid and the base react together to produce water and a chemical called a salt. A wasp sting is basic and can be neutralized with an acid such as lemon juice. A bee or ant sting is acidic and can be neutralized with a base such as baking soda.

A base that dissolves in water is called an alkali. In contrast to acids, alkalis form negative ions when dissolved in water. These are not hydrogen ions, but ions of hydrogen and oxygen, called hydroxide ions.

SALTS

Table salt is just one of many substances called salt. Bath salts are familiar around the home, but there are many other substances that chemists call salts. Many minerals, the natural chemicals rocks are made of, are different kinds of salt.

A salt is a compound that is made when an acid and a base react together. Table salt, for instance, is formed when the base sodium hydroxide neutralizes hydrochloric acid. Acids contain hydrogen and most bases contain metal and oxygen. When a salt forms, the acid's hydrogen swaps with the base's metal, leaving water (hydrogen and oxygen) and the salt (metal plus other elements).

All salts are solids made up of crystals. Crystals of table salt are white and cube-shaped. Some

Salt is often taken out of rock underground by dissolving it with steam. Salty water is then pumped to the surface. The water evaporates, leaving piles of salt.

Did you know?

The human body needs about $\frac{1}{50}$ oz (0.5 g) of salt a day. Most people take in as much as 10 to 20 times this amount with their food, so the kidneys have to filter out the unwanted salt and send it from the body in urine.

salts dissolve in water, like table salt; others won't. Tap water often has traces of dissolved salts, such as calcium carbonate, which make the water "hard." Hard water leaves a crust of limescale around taps and in kettles, and a lot of soap is needed to create a good lather. Some salts, however, make water softer, and some are used in the making of soap.

Salts are used in making a huge range of industrial and agricultural chemicals. The salt ammonium nitrate, for example, is used in fertilizers designed to add nitrogen to the soil. Natural mineral salts are also a source of metals such as sodium and potassium.

Plants and animals depend on various salts to stay alive. Table salt, for example, plays a crucial role in maintaining the body's water balance. The salts sodium chloride and potassium chloride are needed by nerves to send signals.

In focus

COMMON SALT

Table, or common, salt is the chemical compound sodium chloride, and is the most widely used mineral in the world. One expert calculated 16,000 different uses for it, besides in cooking. It is used in the food industry to preserve meat, fish, and vegetables, and also in making things such as margarine and butter. It is also used in making dyes, medicines, pottery, and leather, and it is spread on roads and pavements to keep them free of ice in winter. Most salt comes from thick layers of "rock salt" in the ground, but some is obtained by evaporating seawater.

ACID TESTS

You will need

- ✓ A pitcher
- ✓ A tall glass jar
- ✓ Distilled water
- ✓ A red cabbage
- ✓ Four small glass jars
- ✓ A strainer
- ✓ Acidic and basic test substances (see next page)

1 Finely chop the cabbage and drop it into 1 pint (or 0.5 l) of distilled water. Ask an adult to boil the water for 10 minutes.

In focus

ACID SCALE

Some substances are more acidic than others, and some more basic. In 1909, Danish biochemist Soren Sorensen devised the pH scale for acidity. The letters pH stand for "potential Hydrogen," since the strength of an acid depends on how many hydrogen ions form. The strongest acids have a pH of 1, the strongest bases have a pH of 14. A pH of 7 is neutral, like pure water. Stomach acid has a pH of about 2, lemon juice has a pH of 3, rainwater about 5.5, human blood about 7.4, and ammonia cleaners about 11.

2 Leave the deep-purple liquid to cool for half an hour, then strain it into the tall jar and dispose of the cabbage.

What is happening?

When red cabbage is boiled in pure, distilled water, it becomes an "acid-base indicator." This means it indicates how acidic or basic a substance is by changing color. It is turned red by an acid, changing to violet with a neutral substance, to blue with a weak base, green with a fairly strong base, and yellow with a very strong base. Red cabbage is just one of many natural indicators including geranium petals, blue grapes, and blackberries. Chemists still often use litmus paper. This is paper soaked in litmus—extracted from lichens—then dried. But most now use artificial indicators.

3 To see if a substance is acidic or basic, pour some cabbage liquid into each jar. Then add a little of the test substance.

Basic substances such as ammonia cleaner and washing soda (sodium carbonate) turn the liquid green.

Tap water usually contains impurities that make it slightly alkaline. Like baking soda, it turns the liquid blue.

Distilled water has no impurities and is completely neutral, so it leaves the liquid unchanged in color.

Lemon, vinegar, and cream of tartar powder are all acidic and turn the liquid bright red.

CHEMICAL FORMULA

Using chemical equations, chemists can summarize and even predict what may happen when chemicals react.

Chemicals are named according to the elements they are made of. So aluminum oxide contains aluminum and oxygen. But some everyday chemicals have long names, like sodium hydrogencarbonate (baking soda). Other names are even longer. So chemists use shorthand symbols to identify the various chemical elements.

Often, an element's symbol is just its initial letter. The symbol for oxygen is O, carbon is C, and nitrogen is N. Where two chemicals begin with the same letter, a second small letter is added to distinguish them. So

$3H^+ + 3NO^{3-} \longrightarrow Fe^{3+} + 3NO^{3-} + 3H_2O$

$Fe(OH)_3 + 3H^+ + 3NO^{3-} \longrightarrow Fe^{3+} + 3NO^{3-} + 3H_2O$

Mg_2Si

$A_2 + X_2 \longleftrightarrow 2AX$

$Ba^{2+} + 2OH^- + 2H^+ + 2Cl^- \longrightarrow Ba^{2+} + 2Cl^- + 2H_2O$

$Fe(OH)_3 + 3H^+ + 3NO^{3-} \longrightarrow Fe^{3+} + 3NO^{3-} + 3H_2O$

$A_2 + X_2 \longleftrightarrow 2AX$

$C_6H_{12}O_6$

$NaCl$

H_2O

Ag

6

$C_6H_{12}O_6$

H_2O

NH_3

$Ba^{2+} + 2OH^- +$

CO_2

$NaCH_2SO_4$

Pb_3O_4

$NaCl$

CO_2

Mg_2Si

$2C + O_2 \longleftrightarrow 2CO$

$A_2 + X_2 \longleftrightarrow 2AX$

$H_2O + OH \longleftrightarrow 2H_2O$

$A_2 + X_2 \longleftrightarrow 2AX$

$2C + O_2 \longleftrightarrow 2CO$

$2C + O_2 \longleftrightarrow 2CO$

$Ba^{2+} + 2Cl^- + 2H_2O$

$2Na^+ + S^{2-} \longrightarrow H_2S \ (g) + 2Na^+ + 2Cl^-$

$2H^+ + 2Cl^- + 2Na^+ + S^{2-} \longrightarrow H_2S \ (g) + 2Na^+ + 2Cl^-$

$3NO^{3-} + 3H_2O$

$X_2 \longleftrightarrow 2AX$

$3Ca + N_2$

$A_2 + X_2 \longleftrightarrow 2AX$

$+ O_2 \longleftrightarrow 2CO$

hydrogen is H and helium is He. For chemists, symbols are not just shorthand; they can be combined to make a formula. By adding little numbers to the symbols, a formula can show how many atoms of each element make up a molecule of the chemical.

The symbol for hydrogen is H, but its formula is H_2 because hydrogen molecules have two atoms. With metals, carbon, and some gases, the symbol is the same as the formula, because molecules have a single atom. With nonmetals, such as sulfur (S), the molecules always have two or more atoms. The formula for sulfur is S_8.

It works in the same way for compounds. A molecule of copper oxide is one atom of copper (Cu) plus one of oxygen (O), so the formula for copper oxide is CuO, the same as the symbols. But carbon dioxide molecules have one carbon (C) and two oxygen (O) atoms. So the formula for carbon dioxide is written CO_2.

Some chemical formulas show not only the atoms in a compound, but also the way they are linked together. The order of symbols in the formula for potassium nitrate is KNO_3. This shows the three oxygen atoms are linked not to the potassium (K) but to the nitrogen atom.

CHEMICAL EQUATIONS

A chemical reaction can be described by writing an "equation." This shows the formulas for the reactants (original chemicals) and for the products. It is called an equation because all the atoms that were there before the reaction are still there at the end; they are simply rearranged to form different compounds. When methane (CH_4) reacts with oxygen (O_2), the methane's carbon joins oxygen to make carbon dioxide (CO_2); its hydrogen joins oxygen to form water (H_2O).

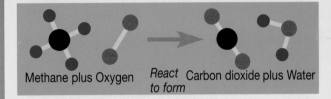

Methane plus Oxygen *React to form* Carbon dioxide plus Water

As a formula, this could be written:
$$CH_4 + O_2 \longrightarrow CO_2 + H_2O$$
This simply shows the chemicals involved, but is not an equation, because two hydrogen atoms seem to have been lost and an oxygen atom gained. In fact, they haven't been lost or gained at all. Experiments show that each molecule of methane reacts not with one molecule of oxygen but two, and the reaction creates not just one molecule of water but two.

So the equation should be written:
$$CH_4 + 2\,O_2 \longrightarrow CO_2 + 2\,H_2O$$
The number of atoms before and after now matches to create a "balanced" equation. Whenever an equation does not balance with equal number of atoms either side, scientists try to work out how many extra molecules are needed to make it balance.

Solids, Liquids, and Gases

Just about all of the universe is empty space—but not all of it. Scattered throughout the universe are tiny bits of stuff called matter.

Matter is every substance in the universe—everything that is not empty space, from the tiniest speck of dust to the most gigantic star. Matter is what we are made of and what the world and everything else in the universe is made of.

Although there is a huge variety of matter, nearly all of it comes in just three basic forms—solid, liquid, and gas. Solids are hard like rock. You can see them and maybe even pick them up. Liquids are like

In this chilly Arctic scene, water exists as a solid (in ice), as liquid (in the sea), and as gas (as water vapor in the air).

Did you know?

The Ancient Greeks thought there were four kinds of matter—fire, air, water, earth—which they called elements. Scientists now know there are more than 100 elements (kinds of atom). But the Greeks' elements are not so different from our three phases of matter—solid (like earth), liquid (like water), and gas (like air).

water. They are harder to see and harder still to pick up without a container. Gases are like air, and often invisible and impossible to pick up.

Every kind of matter can come in these three forms, which scientists call the *states* (or *phases*) of matter. Each kind of matter can change from one state to another, just as ice turns to water when it gets warm, and water turns to steam when it gets hot. An iron bar may melt to a liquid when it gets hot. A drink may freeze solid when it gets cold. It all depends on how hot or cold it is.

In focus

Seen under a microscope, pollen grains in water appear to move by themselves. In fact, they are knocked about by tiny, fast-moving water molecules.

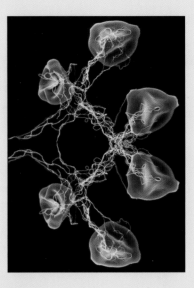

MOVING ATOMS

This book may look solid but, like all the matter in the universe, it's really empty space dotted with incredibly tiny, bits or particles, such as atoms and molecules. Atoms are so small you can see them only with special microscopes. You could fit two billion on the period at the end of this sentence. Atoms join together to make molecules, which are usually only a little bigger.

All kinds of matter, whether solid or liquid or gas, are made from atoms and molecules. These particles are constantly moving very fast. What makes solids, liquids, and gases different is the *way* the particles move. This is called the "kinetic" theory of matter. Kinetic comes from the Greek for "moving."

Particles are so small, and move so fast, that it is impossible to see them moving. But, in 1827, Scottish botanist Robert Brown looked at pollen grains floating in water and saw them moving about. We now know they move because they are being knocked by invisibly small water molecules. This is called Brownian motion.

SOLIDS

Buildings are made from solids, like metal, glass, and stone, because solids are rigid and keep their shape.

Solids are things such as rocks, brick walls, rubber balls, the metal in cars, the bones in your body, and much more. What all solids have in common is that they can be made into particular shapes. Once made into a shape, a solid tends to stay the same shape and size unless forced into a new shape. If a factory makes a brick, for instance, it will usually stay brick shaped.

Some solids, like concrete blocks, are really hard, and it takes a lot of force to change their shape. Other solids, like modeling clay and butter, are soft, and it is quite easy to change their shape.

Did you know?
Diamonds are the world's hardest natural solids. They are so tough that saws with pieces of diamond in their blades can be used to cut through slabs of stone or even solid metal!

In focus

SOLID PARTICLES

Solids keep their shape because the particles they are made of are knitted tightly together. Just like magnetism pulls magnets together, so strong forces between the particles in a solid pull them together and hold them in place. They can vibrate in place, but they cannot move around.

In fact, most solids are "crystalline" (see page 10). This means the particles are knitted together in a pattern, called a lattice, that makes up tiny grains, or crystals. Solids such as glass and plastic, however, are noncrystalline, or "amorphous." In these, the particles are knitted together in a disorderly way. These solids are smooth rather than grainy.

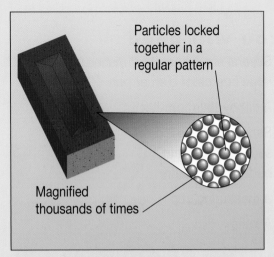

Particles locked together in a regular pattern

Magnified thousands of times

Particles in a solid are held very tightly together in a neat pattern. They are bonded together so firmly that they cannot move, but simply vibrate in place.

All hard solids are difficult to reshape, but some can be broken quite easily—snapping like a twig, or shattering when hit, like china. Such solids are said to be brittle. Brittle solids are almost impossible to reshape; they will break instead of changing shape. But hard solids, such as many metals, are said to be "malleable." This means they can be hammered or beaten into new shapes. The word malleable comes from *malleus*, the Ancient Roman word for hammer.

Some solids, like nylon rope, are soft but difficult to tear apart. Solids like these are said to have great "tensile strength."

Although solids have a particular size and shape most of the time, this is not always the case. Some solids, like tar and chocolate, will bulge into different shapes on warm days without actually melting.

All solids—hard or soft, brittle or malleable—will stay solid only as long as they stay cool enough. As soon as they are warmed above a certain temperature, called the *melting point*, they will melt and become liquid. Each substance has its own melting point. Butter, tar, and chocolate will begin to melt even on a mildly warm day. But the heat of a furnace is needed to melt steel.

MELTING

You will need

- ✓ Several small heatproof dishes plus one large heatproof dish or pan
- ✓ A candy thermometer
- ✓ Samples for testing, such as chocolate, butter, and gelatin
- ✓ A measuring cup
- ✓ A knife

1 Break the samples into small chunks, either by hand or with a knife. Put the chunks in the small heatproof dishes.

In the real world

MELTING POINT

Every substance is solid up to a certain temperature, after which, it melts to a liquid. Once liquid, it freezes (turns solid again) if the temperature drops back past the same point. So the melting point and freezing point are the same temperature. These are some typical melting points:

- Oxygen: -426 °F (-219 °C)
- Water: 32 °F (0 °C)
- Lead: 622 °F (328 °C)
- Iron: 2,802 °F (1,539 °C)
- Tungsten: 6,170 °F (3,410 °C)
- Diamond: 6,332 °F (3,500 °C)

2 Put the large heatproof dish or pan on the stove and pour in water to fill it to a depth of an inch (2 cm) or so.

What is happening?

When a solid substance like gelatin is heated, its particles vibrate faster and faster. Eventually they are vibrating so vigorously that they break the bonds that hold them in place. So the substance melts and becomes a liquid. If it cools again, the particles will vibrate slower and slower until the bonds form one again. This is what happens when a substance freezes.

3 Gently lower two of the sample dishes into the water, taking care that water does not spill into the dishes.

Ask an adult to turn on the burner at a low heat and to supervise the remainder of the experiment. Do not attempt to do this by yourself. Insert the candy thermometer in the water and keep checking the temperature as it slowly heats up. Watch the samples in the dishes and note the temperature of the water when each sample begins to melt. Keep checking, and note the temperature at which each sample is totally melted. When the samples have melted, turn the heat off and wait for the water to cool down. When it is very cold, take out the dishes and repeat the experiment with the other samples.

CRYSTALS

If you look closely at the grains of sugar in a sugar bowl, you will see that they are tiny cubes. These cubes are called sugar crystals. Salt is made of crystals as well, though they are usually much smaller than sugar crystals. Gems such as diamonds and emeralds are crystals too.

In fact, most solids, including metals and rocks, are made up of crystals. You cannot always see the crystals in metal, because they are very small or firmly stuck together. But you can often see them in pieces of rock, if you use a magnifying glass.

Crystals are bits of solids that form in regular, geometrical shapes, with smooth faces and sharp edges. They come in chunks rather than rounded shapes. Many crystals are shiny or clear. They got their name from the glassy chunks of quartz crystal that the Greeks called *krystallos*. They thought it was a special kind of ice that would not melt.

Natural salt crystals have irregular shapes.

Did you know?

In 1880, French scientist Pierre Curie found that some crystals give a small electric current when squeezed. Also, a small electric current applied to these crystals makes them vibrate. This effect is called piezoelectricity. If pressure is applied to quartz crystals, for instance, an electric current or even a spark may be generated. This is how the lighters for gas stoves work. In a quartz watch, which contains a tiny quartz crystal, an electrical current from the watch's battery sets the crystal vibrating at exactly 32,678 times a second. The vibrations keep the watch's electric motor timed so exactly that quartz watches are accurate to within 60 seconds in a year.

Crystals in rocks don't always have a definite shape because they are packed too tightly. But if allowed to form freely in rock cavities, they grow into beautiful regular shapes. Scientists know that crystals get their regular shapes because they are made of atoms linked together in a neat structure, or "lattice."

Perfect crystals only form occasionally. Through careful study, scientists have realized that all crystals build up in one

LIQUID CRYSTALS

Most crystals are solid, but when some special crystals warm up, they don't melt immediately. Instead, they go dark and turn semiliquid. These are called liquid crystals. When they warm up a

Liquid crystals are used for most computers.

little, they flow like a liquid, but their molecules keep some of their neat pattern, so they can hold their shape. The LCDs (liquid crystal displays) you see on computer screens and watches have clear liquid crystals held between two sheets of glass. To make the displays, small electrical currents are used to warm the crystals and make them go dark in exactly the right pattern.

of six basic shapes or "systems," such as in cubes, flat plates, or hexagonal rods. Each system reflects the crystal's lattice of atoms. By shining X rays through the crystal, scientists can analyze the lattice structure. This is called X-ray crystallography. Scientists used X-ray crystallography in the 1950s to discover the structure of DNA, the basic chemical in every cell that carries all of the instructions for life.

MAKING CRYSTALS

You will need

- ✔ A small saucepan
- ✔ A plastic storage container
- ✔ Food coloring
- ✔ A measuring pitcher
- ✔ A wooden spoon
- ✔ Sugar

1 Pour ½ cup (0.25 l) of water into a pan. Stir in 1 cup (0.5 l) of sugar. Ask an adult to heat the pan until the sugar dissolves.

In the real world

BLACK GLASS

Most rocks are made of crystals, but the crystals are often so small they can only be seen with a microscope. One exception is obsidian, which forms in small pockets when lava cools so quickly crystals have no time to form. The result is a shiny, black, glasslike rock.

Obsidian was prized by Native Americans long ago. They used it to make arrowheads.

2 Allow the liquid to cool and stir in drops of food coloring. Pour the liquid into a plastic container and leave for two days.

3 Push the crystals on the surface down into the liquid with a spoon. Leave for a week, then drain off any excess liquid.

What is happening?

Rock candy forms in the same way as igneous rocks. When water is hot, it can dissolve a lot of sugar. But as it cools, less sugar can stay dissolved. So some begins to turn solid. As it turns solid the sugar grows into crystals, because one bit of sugar is drawn to another. As the water evaporates over the week, ever more sugar crystallizes. The same happens as molten magma cools to form igneous rock. Here, dissolved minerals rather than sugar slowly crystallize out of the liquid. The more gradual this crystallization is, the bigger the crystals grow. Rocks that cool slowly far underground form the biggest crystals.

When the crystals are dry, turn the container upside down and push the base to break them into chunks. Turn the resulting rock candy out on to a bowl or sheet of wax paper. The crystals you get may be quite small, and people argue about the best way to get big crystals like those in the picture. The key is to leave the liquid to cool undisturbed as long and slowly as possible. You could also try adding a few large grains or chunks of sugar to act as "seeds" around which crystals will grow.

LIQUIDS

The most common liquid by far is water. But soft drinks, oil, wine, and milk are all liquids. Unlike solids, liquids cannot hold their shape. In fact, they flow into the shape of any container they are poured into.

All liquids flow, but some flow more easily than others. Oil flows slower than water, and thick paint flows slower still. A liquid's resistance to flow—its stickiness—is called its viscosity.

Although liquids flow into any shape, unlike gases, liquids always have a definite surface. Whenever

Milk is a special kind of liquid called a suspension. Solid fat particles are suspended within it.

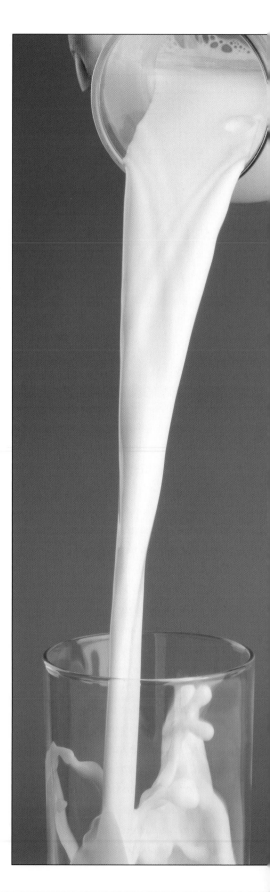

In focus

When a solid melts and becomes a liquid, many of the bonds holding the molecules together break, so clusters of them wander in all directions. This is why liquids flow into any shape. Particles in a solid are like ranks of soldiers marching on the spot. Those in a liquid are more like dancers on a crowded dancefloor.

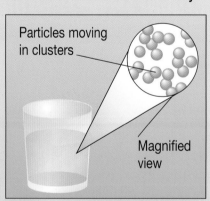

Particles moving in clusters

Magnified view

Clusters of molecules in a liquid such as water wander freely in all directions.

Did you know?

SLIDING FREELY

Solids do not usually have slippery surfaces. Even ice is not slippery. So why do ice cubes slip from your fingers, and how can skaters zoom over the ice? The answer is that the surface of the ice is lubricated by a thin layer of water. When you pick up an ice cube, the warmth of your fingers melts the ice to create a layer of water. When a skater zooms over the ice, the pressure of the skate blades melts water beneath them.

It looks as if skaters are zooming around on solid ice. In fact, they are traveling on water, melted by the pressure of the skate.

a liquid is poured into a container, its top surface is smooth and flat. In fact, if you pour a liquid in a container with several branches, it rises up to the same level in each branch.

Actually, the surface of a liquid is not always quite flat. If you look closely at the top of a glass filled to the brim with water, you will notice that the surface of the water curves up over the edge at the top of the glass. This bowing, called a meniscus, is due to an effect called surface tension. It is caused by the molecules in a liquid pulling together. When a bit of water falls through the air, it is surface tension that pulls the water into round drops.

When a liquid is heated, some molecules break free of the surface as the heat makes them move faster. The molecules that break free form a gas. Some form bubbles within the liquid, but most drift away from the liquid's surface. This is called evaporation. Once the liquid reaches the boiling point, it won't get any hotter; it just evaporates. Steam is tiny drops of evaporated water in the air. If the gas that has evaporated from a liquid cools down, it turns back into a liquid, often forming little droplets on cold surfaces. This is called condensation. Dew is water condensed from the air in the cool of the night.

LIQUID POWER

You will need

- ✓ A large plastic bowl
- ✓ Length of plastic tubing to fit on syringe
- ✓ Two syringes (such as for icing cakes)
- ✓ Waterproof tape (to seal joints)

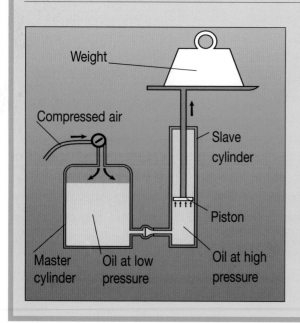

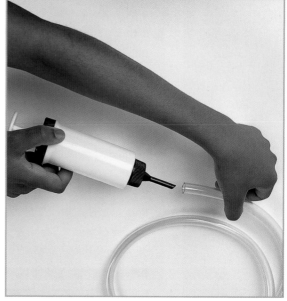

1 Screw the nozzle of the syringes on as tightly as you can, then insert one of them into the end of the plastic tube.

In the real world

HYDRAULIC POWER

Hydraulic machines use liquids such as oil to transmit power as in this experiment. They have a "master" cylinder, like the syringe you push in, and a "slave," like the one pushed out. They gain immense power by transferring a liquid from a larger, master, cylinder to a smaller slave. In this diagram of a hydraulic lift, the large piston is actually compressed air. This pushes a large volume of oil in the master into the narrower, slave cylinder. The effort applied to the master is hugely concentrated and multiplied in the slave, forcing out the piston and lifting the load that it is carrying.

Weight

Compressed air

Slave cylinder

Piston

Master cylinder

Oil at low pressure

Oil at high pressure

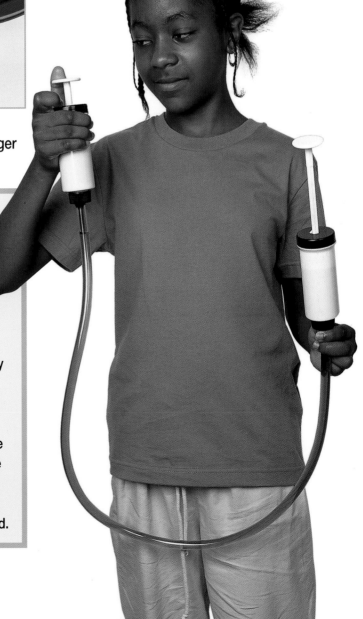

Make sure the plunger of the other syringe is pushed in, then insert its nozzle, under water, into the other end of the tube.
Now lift both plungers and the tube out of the water. Press in the plunger that is out, and you should see the other plunger move out.

2 Immerse the tube and syringe in a bowl of water, and pull out the plunger to draw water in.

What is happening?

Liquids may flow very easily, but, unlike gas, they cannot be squashed into a smaller space. In a gas, the particles are far apart and can be squeezed closer together. But in a liquid, although the particles are only loosely linked, they are so close together that they cannot be squeezed any closer—it is impossible to squeeze a liquid very much. Liquids are said to be incompressible.
So, in this experiment, when you push one plunger in, the water must move down the tube because it cannot be squeezed.
As the water moves down the tube, it pushes the other plunger out the other end.

GASES

Gases can be difficult to detect. The air all around you is made of gases, yet you cannot see them because they are transparent. You cannot feel gases either—except how warm or cold they are. You cannot pick them up or hold them. In fact, gases have no shape at all. They simply spread out to fill the whole container, no matter what size it is.

Indeed, the only way you would even be aware of many gases is from their smell. Some gases have a strong smell, like hydrogen sulfide, which smells like rotten eggs. But some gases, like the natural gas used for cooking and heating,

Gases spread out to fill any space—like the air you blow into a balloon. You can't see the air, but, as the balloon expands, you can tell that it is filling up with more air.

Did you know?

Gas particles move very quickly. This why you can smell a perfume almost the instant someone enters a room—the scent particles spread rapidly among the air particles and a few of them reach your nose. This process, in which gas particles mix with each other, is called diffusion.

do not even smell much. This is why gas companies often add another gas with an odor to the gas supply so that people can smell a gas leak.

Although gases are hard to pin down, they are matter, just like solids and liquids. Each gas has its own characteristics. Gases are very light and thin, but even the lightest gas, hydrogen, can be weighed. Some gases have their own color, such as nitrogen dioxide, which is brown.

In focus

MOVING PARTICLES

Particles in a gas are not at all held together. They move around freely and crash into each other at high speed.

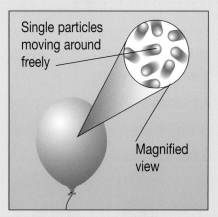

Single particles moving around freely

Magnified view

The particles in a gas are far apart, which is why gases are so light and hard to see. There are trillions of particles in just a thimbleful of gas, but they are so small they fill only about a thousandth of the space. These particles constantly bounce around, colliding into each other billions of times a second. If a gas is cooled, the particles slow down, and the gas condenses to become a liquid, just as steam from a kettle condenses to water drops on a cold surface.

In the real world

GASES IN THE AIR

The air around you is a mixture of gases. Most air (99 percent) is made up of just two gases: nitrogen and oxygen. More than three-quarters (78 percent) is nitrogen; only 21 percent is oxygen. But the oxygen is vital—all animals, including humans, need to breathe oxygen to stay alive. Fires need oxygen to burn. The remaining one percent of the air is carbon dioxide, water vapor, and traces of other gases, such as neon, helium, ozone, and krypton.

GASES AND VOLUME

You will need

- ✔ Baking soda
- ✔ White vinegar
- ✔ A small glass bottle
- ✔ A balloon
- ✔ A tablespoon
- ✔ A funnel

1 Use the funnel to fill the balloon with baking soda. Then pour ½ inch (1.2 cm) of vinegar into the bottle.

In focus

GAS LAW

Gases exert a push, or "pressure," on the things they meet. This is created by the combined impact of all the gas's moving particles. The more particles there are, the greater the pressure. Irish scientist Robert Boyle (1627–1691) showed that when you squeeze a gas, the pressure goes up in proportion, as long as the temperature stays the same. This is because you are squeezing more particles into a smaller space. If you heat up a gas but keep it in exactly the same sized container, its pressure goes up because the particles move faster. This is Boyle's Law.

2 Keeping the balloon hanging down, stretch its neck over the neck of the bottle as far as it will go.

What is happening?

Mixing baking soda with an acid like vinegar starts a vigorous chemical reaction that releases carbon dioxide. The gas takes up much more space than the solid and the liquid, so it inflates the balloon.

As soon as the balloon is securely stretched over the bottle, quickly lift it upright. Shake the balloon so that the soda drops straight down into the vinegar below. As soon as the soda meets the vinegar, it will start to fizz and froth rapidly and the balloon will inflate.

In the real world

WATER IN THE AIR

Like a wet sponge, the air is full of water. You can't see it, though, because water in the air is in the form of an invisible gas called water vapor. It forms as water evaporates from oceans and lakes. Air with water vapor in it is called humid. As humid air gets warmer, it expands and can hold more water, because there are bigger spaces between particles. When humid air cools, the spaces between the particles become smaller so the air cannot take in any more vapor. It is said to be saturated. The temperature at which this happens is called dew point. If it gets cooler still, the vapor will condense to form dew, fog or clouds.

Dew is drops of water that condense out of the warm air when the temperature drops to the dew point.

CHANGING PHASES

You will need

- ✓ Two plastic ice trays
  (for making ice in a freezer)
- ✓ Table salt
- ✓ A pitcher of water
- ✓ A spoon

1 Stir table salt into the pitcher of water. At first, it will all dissolve. Keep on adding salt until no more will dissolve.

Did you know?

Heating a substance does not always simply raise its temperature. When a solid melts or a liquid evaporates, just that little extra heat is needed to break the bonds between particles. Scientists call this extra heat latent heat. When a solid is at melting point, heat does not raise its temperature. Instead, it provides the latent heat needed to break the bonds between particles. As the bonds break, the solid melts. Similarly, when a liquid evaporates, it takes away extra heat from its surroundings. This is why sweating helps keep you cool. Sweat is warm water that evaporates from your skin. As sweat evaporates, it draws heat from your skin and so cools you.

2 Pour the salted water into one of the ice trays. Fill the other tray with plain water. Place both trays in the freezer.

After about five hours, take the ice trays from the freezer. Closely examine them. You will find the tray of plain water has turned entirely to solid ice. The salt water in the other tray will be only partially frozen, or not frozen at all—unless your freezer is set to a very low temperature.

MIXTURES AND SOLUTIONS

Some substances are made of just one pure chemical, like pure gold and pure water. But most, such as milk, oil, the air, and most foods, are mixtures of different chemicals. The various chemicals in a mixture may be thoroughly mixed up, but they do not ever interact.

Like different marbles in a box, their molecules remain intact, and it is often possible to separate them from each other.

Water from the tap usually looks clear and pure. But even the cleanest tap water is actually a mixture, with traces of various other substances. In fact, tap

Seawater is a solution. Only about 96.5 percent is actually water. The rest is dissolved chemicals, mainly salts such as sodium chloride.

Did you know?

The blood that flows through your body is made of millions of tiny blood cells in a liquid, called plasma, but it is not the same as gas plasma. Blood plasma is a solution, with many different substances, including proteins, dissolved in water.

water is a very particular kind of mixture called a solution.

In a solution, a solid, liquid, or gas (the solute) is dissolved in a liquid (the solvent). The molecules of the solute mingle so well with the molecules of the liquid that the solid vanishes. When you make instant coffee by pouring hot water on coffee powder, you are making a solution. The powder is the solute and the water the solvent.

As you dissolve more of the solute in a solvent, the solution becomes stronger and more concentrated. Eventually,

In focus

SUSPENSIONS

Emulsion paint is made of tiny specks of paint suspended in water. This type of suspension is called a "colloidal" suspension.

Water with specks of mud floating in it is not a solution, but a special type of liquid called a suspension—because the mud is not dissolved but suspended in the water. Milk is a suspension, too, but the fat particles suspended in it are far too small to see except under a microscope. Suspensions with such tiny particles are called colloids.

though, it will become saturated and no more will dissolve. You can, however, make a saturated solution absorb more by heating it. Heating expands the solution, increasing the space between its molecules and making more room for the solute to dissolve.

If a saturated solution is cooled or left to evaporate, it actually becomes more than saturated. Then the solute molecules may begin to link up so that crystals grow.

FINDING THE SOLUTION

You will need

✔ Tea bags

✔ A mug

✔ A deep saucer

✔ Sugar cubes

✔ Granulated sugar

✔ A teaspoon

1 Fill up a mug with warm water, adding the last few drops carefully so that the water bulges but does not overflow.

Now try this

Solubility tells us how much of a substance will dissolve in a liquid. The warmer a solution is, the more you can dissolve in it. You can prove this by counting how many lumps of sugar you can stir into a cup of cold tea before no more will dissolve. Now count how many lumps you can stir into a lukewarm cup of tea. Finally, count how many you can add to a cup of hot tea. More lumps will dissolve in the hot tea than in the cold tea. This is because solubility increases with the temperature.

Test the effect of temperature on solubility with cups of tea and some sugar lumps.

2 Very, very carefully, pour a spoonful of sugar into the water and wait for the sugar to dissolve.

Go on adding more sugar bit by bit, waiting for it to dissolve each time. You will probably find you can add three or four more spoonfuls of sugar before the mug finally overflows.

What is happening?

The particles in a liquid are not packed as tightly together as they are in a solid: there is actually a bit of space between them, and solids can dissolve into these spaces. When you add sugar to what seems like a full mug, it does not overflow, because the sugar slips into the spaces between the water particles. In warm water, there are bigger spaces between the particles than in cold water. This is why you can dissolve quite a bit of sugar in it. Only when all the spaces are full, will the water finally spill over the top of the mug.

THE FOURTH STATE

Whenever you see a bolt of lightning flash through the air, you are seeing gases being ionized. The massive heat and electrical surge is enough to ionize the surrounding air instantly.

On Earth, nearly all matter exists either as a solid, a liquid, or a gas. But, out in space, all of these are quite rare. In fact, 99 percent of all matter in the universe exists in a fourth state, called a plasma, which is found very rarely here on Earth.

A plasma is formed when a gas is heated up to an extremely high temperature or shot through with a powerful electrical current. The effect of the heat or electricity is to strip tiny particles called electrons off some of the gas's atoms. This loss of electrons makes them electrically charged, so plasmas buzz with electricity.

Electrically charged atoms are called ions, so plasmas are often called ionized gases. As a plasma gets hotter or the electrical current gets stronger, more atoms become "ionized."

On Earth, the huge electrical charge of a lightning bolt ionizes the air, making it glow. So do even small electrical sparks. In fact, wherever you see a brilliant, cold electrical flash, the air is being turned into a plasma.

Out in space, the Sun and every star in the universe are turned into plasmas by the immense heat of the nuclear reactions going on inside them. The Sun is so hot that streams of plasma radiate throughout the solar system. This is known as solar wind.

Scientists hope to use plasmas to generate electricity one day, by controlling "nuclear fusion," the same process that goes on inside stars. The heat generated from this process can reach 212,000,000 °F (100,000,000 °C), and would melt any container. But, as in a star, the reaction could instead be contained inside a plasma.

Water

Water is so common on Earth that we almost take it for granted. It is by far the most common substance on the face of the earth, and you can find it almost everywhere. Water covers almost three-quarters of the world's surface.

Water fills the oceans, rivers, and lakes. It is in the ground. It is in the air we breathe. It is in our bodies. It is fortunate that water is so common, because water is vital to life. There are no living things on Earth that can survive without a regular supply of water. If you

The water from this waterfall nourishes all the wildlife around it.

Did you know?

THE NEED FOR WATER

Humans can live without food for more than two months, but they can only survive without water for about a week. If the body loses more than 20 percent of its normal water content, a person will die. Humans need about 2½ quarts (2.4 liters) of water a day. This intake can be in the form of beverages or water in food.

let a houseplant dry out, it wilts and dies very quickly. In fact, every living thing consists mostly of water. Your body is about two-thirds water. Many plants are about four-fifths water. Most scientists believe that life itself began in water—in the salty water of the sea.

In the real world

Scientists once thought water was an element, one of the basic chemicals of the universe. In fact, water is a compound (combination) of two gases—oxygen and hydrogen. This was first discovered in 1783 by British scientist Henry Cavendish.

Cavendish used a spark to set fire to a mixture of air and hydrogen gas inside a glass jar. The hydrogen burned up quickly, but Cavendish saw that drops of water had formed on the glass. When he weighed the jar he found that it weighed exactly the same as it had at the start of the experiment.

Cavendish realized that the hydrogen had not escaped at all. In fact, it had joined with oxygen in the air to form water. Careful measurement showed Cavendish that water was made from twice as much hydrogen as oxygen. This is why water has the chemical formula H_2O.

WATER IN THE BODY

You will need

✔ A clear plastic bag (big enough to put your hand inside)

✔ Adhesive tape

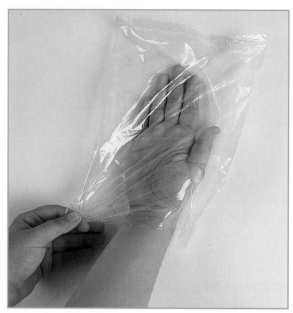

1 Slip your left hand inside a plastic bag (your right, if you are left-handed). Pull up the bag beyond your wrist.

What is happening?

Sweat is salty water that oozes from tiny pores in your skin called sweat glands. As sweat evaporates on the skin, it draws heat from the body. The evaporation cools the body down. That is why people sweat more when they exercise.

2 Fold the top edges of the bag tightly around your wrist. Now tape the edges together to make sure no air gets in.

Now try this

Blow on your finger. You feel the air blowing over it, but because your breath is quite warm, it does not feel cold. Now lick your finger and blow over it again. Suddenly, the breath seems like a chill wind. Why? Your breath has become no colder, but the moisture on your finger is evaporating—changing from a liquid to a gas. Evaporation requires heat, and the heat comes from your finger, which is why your finger suddenly feels cold.

Lick your finger wet, then try blowing on it. You will find it suddenly feels chilled.

After a while, the inside of the bag starts to steam up. The longer you leave it, the more it will steam up. Eventually, drops of water will form on the inside of the bag. This water is sweat coming out of the skin of your hand. Skin is producing sweat most of the time, but it normally stays dry, because the sweat evaporates into the air. The moisture that evaporates from your hand cannot escape from the bag, so it condenses (turns back to liquid) on the inside of the bag.

ICE, WATER, AND STEAM

When liquid water is heated, it boils. The water turns into a gas called water vapor. When the vapor molecules meet cold air, some form tiny droplets of liquid. We see these droplets as steam.

Did you know?

People often confuse steam and water vapor. Water vapor is the gas formed when water evaporates completely and is invisible. Steam is the tiny drops of water that you can see drifting up off hot water.

1.8L
MAX

1.5L

1.0L

0.5L
MIN

In the real world

Water expands when it freezes, so a certain volume of water freezes to make a larger volume of ice. This means that ice is actually less dense (lighter) than water, so ice floats on water. This is why when chunks of ice snap off the end of glaciers into the Arctic Ocean, they do not sink. Instead, they float away as large chunks of ice called icebergs. Because ice is only slightly less dense than water, the iceberg sinks deep into the water. Only the very tip of the iceberg shows above the surface. This makes icebergs very dangerous for ships that accidentally bump into them, like the *Titanic*, which sank when it hit an iceberg on its first voyage in 1912.

If it gets cold enough, liquid water freezes and turns to solid ice. If it gets hot enough, water boils and turns into a gas called water vapor.

This is one of the special things about water. Other substances turn from solid to liquid and from liquid to gas if they are heated. For most materials, this only happens at extreme temperatures. Iron, for instance, does not melt until the temperature is over 2,732 °F (1,500 °C). It does not boil until the temperature soars over a roasting 4,892 °F (2,700 °C).

Water changes from solid to liquid to gas at everyday temperatures. Pure water melts at 32 °F (0 °C) and boils at 212 °F (100 °C). If there are any impurities, the melting and boiling points change. This is one way of testing to see if a liquid is pure water.

Did you know?

SPECIAL BONDS

Water stays liquid until it gets very warm. A lot of energy has to be added to liquid water before the molecules can break apart and form a gas. The reason water stays liquid for so long is because pairs of its molecules are held together by special bonds. These bonds are called hydrogen bonds. Just as opposite poles of a magnet attract each other, the opposite sides of two water molecules stick together. Only when it gets very warm do these bonds break apart, allowing water to turn to gas.

WATER AND ICE

You will need

- ✓ A refrigerator with a freezer
- ✓ A strong plastic cup and saucer
- ✓ A heavy weight, large enough to rest on the cup
- ✓ A measuring cup

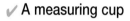

1 Using the measuring cup, fill the plastic cup to the brim with water. Rest the cup on the saucer.

In focus

WATER MOLECULES

A molecule of water is the tiniest bit of water that exists. Each water molecule has two hydrogen atoms and one oxygen atom. A water molecule is shaped like a flattened V, with the two hydrogen atoms on each tip and the oxygen atom in the middle. Scientists describe water molecules as polar. This is because one "pole" or side of the molecule, the oxygen side, has a slightly negative electrical charge. The other side has a slightly positive electrical charge. The attractions between the positive pole on one molecule and the negative pole on another molecule are called hydrogen bonds.

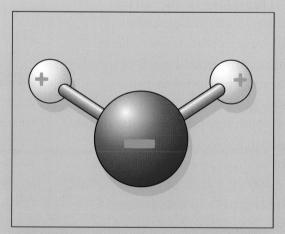

This diagram shows the V-shape of a water molecule. The oxygen atom is shown in red, and the two hydrogen atoms in white.

When most substances freeze from liquid to solid, they shrink. Unlike most other substances, water expands as it freezes. In other words, a certain volume of water freezes to make a slightly larger volume of ice, which is why the ice fills the jug higher than the water. In fact, when it freezes, water swells with enormous power—enough power to lift the weight. This can cause a problem in household water pipes. In cold winters, water can expand inside pipes as it freezes and burst the pipes.

2 Place the weight on top of the cup. Now carefully carry the cup and saucer and put them inside the freezer.

Leave overnight, then take the cup out of the freezer. You will see that the ice has lifted the weight above the edge of the cup.

WATER IN THE WORLD

Nearly all the water in the world, 97.25 percent, is the salt water of the oceans. Most of the rest of the world's water, 2.05 percent, is locked away in the frozen polar ice caps and in glaciers. Less than 1 percent of the water on Earth is freshwater in lakes and rivers, springs, and under ground. An even tinier proportion exists as rain, snow, and water vapor in the air.

Most freshwater lies under the ground. Only about 0.02 percent of freshwater is found in rivers and lakes.

Did you know?

If you have ever tasted seawater, you know it tastes salty. This is because seawater is only 96.5 percent pure water. Dissolved in it, like sugar in a cup of coffee, are billions of tons of salts. By far the most common salt is sodium chloride, table salt. Seawater also contains other ingredients such as magnesium, sulfur, calcium, and potassium.

Most ocean water stays in the oceans, circulating round and round as the ocean waters are warmed by the Sun and blown by the wind.

Freshwater is continually changing places, moving among the oceans, the air, and the land in an endless cycle. The technical word for anything to do with water is hydrology, and scientists call this cycle of freshwater the hydrological cycle or water cycle.

There is a huge amount of water in the world. But the human need for water is great, and the water does not always exist where it is needed. As the world's population grows, our need for water grows too. In the year 2000, the world demand for freshwater was almost double what it was in the 1980s. Rich countries such as the United States and those in Europe use huge amounts of water. The average European uses 6,340 pints (3,000 liters) of water a day; the average African uses just 4.2 pints (2 liters). Some countries regularly suffer droughts and water shortages, and no country is completely safe from finding itself short of water.

THE HYDROLOGICAL CYCLE

The world's freshwater is being recycled all the time. Every second of the day, a huge amount of new water vapor is joining the air as it evaporates from oceans and lakes or transpires from plants. Warm air currents then lift the vapor high up where the air gets cooler. As the air cools, the vapor condenses (turns to drops of water) or freezes into tiny ice crystals, forming clouds. The water drops and ice crystals in clouds grow bigger as more water vapor floats up. Soon they grow so big they become too heavy to float on the air, and they fall back to the ground or into the oceans as rain or snow. This is called precipitation. When rain or snow falls on the ground, it either soaks in and is taken up by plants, or it runs in rivers back to lakes and the oceans, ready to evaporate again.

Water falls as rain, snow, or sleet

Hot air rises

The hydrological cycle shows the constant flow of Earth's water. The whole cycle is powered by the heat of the Sun.

CLOUDS AND HUMIDITY

You might not know it, but you are walking around in a sea of water. Like a sponge, air soaks up invisible water vapor. All air near the ground contains some water vapor, but just how much it holds—the air's humidity—depends on how hot and dry the weather is. Water gets into the air because the

Dark layers of clouds usually mean that a storm is coming.

Did you know?

As the air cools down, it holds less water. After a cool night, leaves and grass are often covered in drops of water that the air could not hold. This is called dew.

Sun heats up oceans and lakes. Millions of gallons of water then rise into the air as water vapor. This process is called evaporation. As the moist air full of water vapor rises, it cools.

Eventually, when the vapor is high in the air, it gets so cool that the moisture turns into a mist of water droplets, or ice crystals if it is very cold. We see these collections of droplets and ice crystals as clouds.

In focus

CLOUDS

Clouds come in all shapes and sizes, but all are made of billions of tiny water drops or ice crystals. There are three basic types—fluffy white heaped "cumulus" clouds, huge blanket layers of "stratus" clouds, and wispy "cirrus" clouds.

Weather experts also identify the different clouds according to how high they are in the sky ("cirro-", "alto-", or "nimbo-" for high, medium, or low). So altocumulus clouds, for instance, are fluffy cumulus clouds at medium-high altitude while cirrostratus are high, flat clouds. Some clouds, such as stratocumulus and cirrocumulus ("mackerel" skies) are mixtures of two of the three basic types.

Dark gray rain clouds are given the name nimbus. So nimbostratus are layered rainclouds, while cumulonimbus are huge, piled-up thunderclouds.

Cirrus (high, wispy clouds formed from ice) often warn of storms ahead.

Stratocumulus are layers of cumulus, forming in unsettled weather.

Cumulus may grow into towering clouds if there are rising air currents.

Thundery cumulonimbus, the tallest clouds, often stretch into anvil shapes.

A WET AND DRY HYGROMETER

You will need

- ✔ Two identical thermometers
- ✔ Marker pens and ruler
- ✔ A square of plywood
- ✔ A spray can lid
- ✔ Cotton cloth
- ✔ Balsa wood
- ✔ A notebook
- ✔ Glue

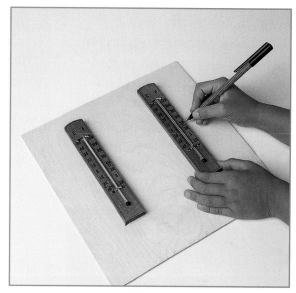

1 Position the thermometers on the board, with bulbs level, and use a pen to mark the temperature scale onto the board down one side of each of the thermometers.

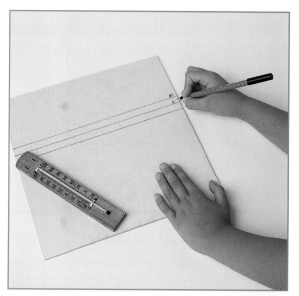

2 Mark the scale right across the board. Glue a strip of balsa wood to the back edge of the board to make a stand. Glue blocks to the back of the thermometers.

Take it further

HUMIDITY READINGS

Scientists have worked out the maximum humidity of the air (the total amount of water vapor it can hold) at different temperatures. They have drawn up charts that show how humid the air is for the different temperature readings on a wet and dry hygrometer. If you have one of these charts (called humidity tables) at school, use your readings to look up the relative humidity. The total amount of moisture in the air is called its "absolute" humidity. But the warmer air is, the more water vapor it can hold—so warm air may hold a lot of water, but still seem dry. Relative humidity is the amount of moisture in the air relative to the total amount it could hold.

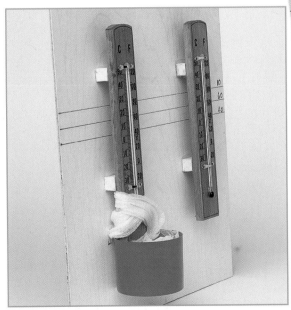

What is happening?

The bulb at the base of one thermometer is in the damp cloth. As the water evaporates from the cloth, it cools the bulb down, so it always gives a slightly lower temperature reading than the other thermometer. In humid weather there will be less evaporation than in dry weather.

3 Stick the thermometers and the lid to the board so one of the bulbs is in the lid. Wind damp cloth around the bulb.

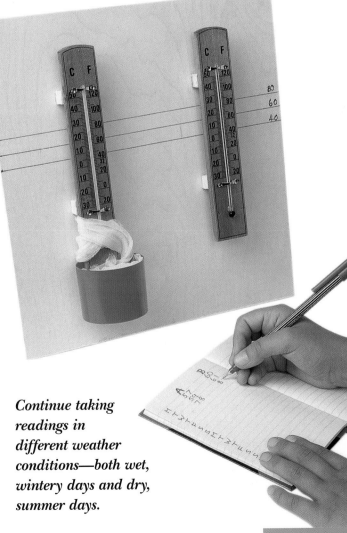

4 Take readings from both thermometers once a day at the same time, and draw a chart to compare the readings.

Continue taking readings in different weather conditions—both wet, wintery days and dry, summer days.

RAIN AND STORMS

Rain is drops of water falling from clouds. But clouds do not always make rain, even though they are full of tiny water droplets and ice crystals.

Most of the droplets in clouds are so tiny and light that they float on air. It only rains when these droplets grow at least a hundred times bigger than normal and get so heavy the air can no longer hold them up.

Cloud drops grow big enough to fall as rain when air is forced to rise suddenly and cools so much that lots of water condenses. Air is forced to rise enough to make rain in three

Lightning occurs when electrical charges build up in clouds and then discharge, like a static shock from metal furniture on a giant scale.

Did you know?

The wettest places in the world are Tutunendo in Colombia and Mount Waialeale, Hawaii, where they get, on average, 460 inches (1,170 cm) of rain a year. This would be enough to flood the region deeper than a two-storey house if the water collected!

main ways: on rising currents of warm air; by being forced up over wedges of warm air at a "front"; and when it runs up against hills and mountains.

The faster that air is driven upward, the heavier the rain will be. The heaviest rain comes from giant cumulonimbus clouds created by strong upward currents of warm air, as seen on hot summer afternoons, especially in the tropics. The layered nimbostratus clouds found along "warm" fronts, on the other hand, tend to give long showers of steady rain.

Even when forced up sharply, the water drops do not fall as rain straight away. First they have to grow even bigger. In warm tropical clouds, they grow by colliding with each other. In cooler clouds, they may start as ice crystals that attract water to them to form snow flakes. The flakes fall into warmer air and melt, then fall as rain.

In focus

MAKING RAINDROPS

Cloud droplets only fall as rain when they become big enough to overcome air resistance. You can see how this happens very simply by spraying water on a window pane or mirror. The droplets will cling on to the glass and not run down until they are large enough. Here the obstacle is surface tension. In a cloud it is air resistance.

Use a liquid spray to mist water evenly over a window pane or mirror. At first the drops are small and create a mist.

As you continue to spray, you will see the water start to form rivers as the drops join together and run down the glass.

HOW TO MEASURE RAINFALL

You will need

- ✔ A 2-pint (1-liter) plastic soft drink bottle with straight sides
- ✔ Small plastic bottle, such as a shampoo bottle
- ✔ Marker pen and ruler
- ✔ Measuring cup
- ✔ Scissors
- ✔ Stones

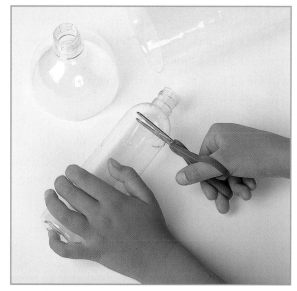

1 Cut the top off the soft drink bottle in a straight line with the scissors: cut around the bottle below the point where it starts to taper. Cut the top off the shampoo bottle.

2 Mark a line on the shampoo bottle above the base. Make another mark ½ in (1 cm) higher up. Fill the bottle to the lower mark. Measure the amount of water.

3 Fill the bottle to the second mark and measure the amount. The difference between these two amounts is the equivalent of ½ in (1 cm) of rain.

4 Pour the measured ½ in (1 cm) into the shampoo bottle and mark the level. Add the same amount of water and make another mark. Repeat up the bottle.

What is happening?

The lid of the bottle acts as a funnel and prevents the rainwater from evaporating before you have taken a reading. Compare your readings with the figures given by the professionals for your region. If your figures are different, see if you can find out why.

5 Place a layer of stones in the large bottle. Stand the small bottle upright in the stones. Turn the top of the large bottle upside down to make a funnel.

6 Stand the rain gauge outdoors, 1 ft (30 cm) above the ground. Check the level of water in the small bottle daily, then empty it. Record the daily rainfall.

WATER POWER

If you have ever stood under a waterfall or been bowled over by a big wave from the sea, you know that water has immense power when it is moving. Sometimes water's power comes from its momentum. Big waves are very hard to stop because there is such a weight of water in them. Other times water's power comes from its depth, since pressure—the water's power to push—increases with depth. Sometimes the power comes from gravity, as when rivers flow downhill to turn a water wheel or turbine.

The amount of power water generates when it is flowing downhill depends on its pressure. The pressure depends on the weight of water pushing down. Hydrologists talk of a "head" of water. This is really

Surfers are using the power of water when they ride the ocean waves.

In focus

Hydroelectric power (HEP) plants use moving water to turn turbines to generate electricity. Typically a huge dam is constructed. The power plant is often inside the base of the dam, where the pressure is greatest. Sluice gates open to let water gush through a tunnel to the plant's turbine. As the water rushes through the turbine, it spins the turbine blades, and the turbine drives the electric generator.

HEP plants are expensive to build. But once they are working, they are cheaper to run than oil and coal power stations and they do not pollute the air. At present, HEP accounts for about 20 percent of the world's electric power and about 9 percent of the electricity produced in the United States.

In the real world

WATERMILLS

Watermills are the simplest and oldest power plants, dating back at least to the time of the Romans. They have a wheel with paddles that are turned by water flowing either under them (undershot wheels) or over the top (overshot wheels). Until the Industrial Revolution in Britain, watermills were used mainly for grinding corn. They were also used in ancient China to blow bellows for metal-working. When the Industrial Revolution came in the mid-18th century, huge water wheels were used to power machines in the first factories.

Until the invention of the steam engine, people relied on water power. This watermill in France was used to grind corn.

just the depth of water creating the pressure. The deeper the water, the greater the head and the greater the pressure at the bottom. A cubic foot (0.028 cubic m) of water weighs 62.4 pounds (28 kg), so water 100 feet (30.5 m) deep creates a pressure of 62.4 times 100 or 6,240 pounds per square foot at the bottom. Water would shoot out of a pipe through a dam 100 feet below the surface at over 80 feet per second.

To use water power, hydrologists try to create a large head or depth of water by damming up a river in a pond or lake. In old-fashioned watermills, they built a millpond. In modern hydroelectric power plants, they often build a huge dam.

HOW TO MAKE A TOY DIVER

You will need

- ✔ A tall glass jar with a wide neck
- ✔ A small plastic pen cap
- ✔ Thin, strong string
- ✔ A small sheet of thin rubber
- ✔ Re-usable poster putty

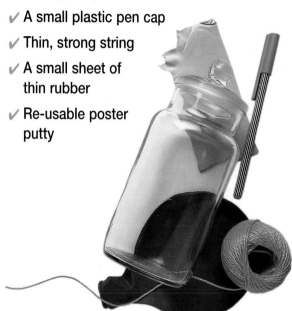

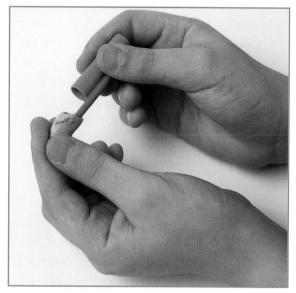

1 Fill the jar with water almost to the top. Fix a small lump of poster putty to the tip of the pocket clip on the pen cap to make the pen cap float upright.

In focus

You can see how water pressure increases with depth with this simple experiment. Cut the top off a plastic bottle. Make a row of three holes up the side of the bottle, 2 in (5 cm) apart. Cover the holes tightly with your fingers. Ask a friend to fill the bottle with water. Once the bottle is full, take away your fingers, all at once. The water trickles from the top hole and shoots out farther from the middle. It jets out most powerfully from the lowest hole because the pressure is greatest here.

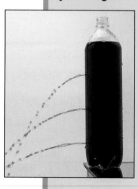

2 Float the pen cap, point up, in a bowl of water. Add or remove poster putty until it floats just below the surface. Now lower the cap into the jar.

What is happening?

The pen cap and poster putty are kept afloat by the bubble of air trapped inside the cap. When you press on the rubber, you increase the pressure of the water in the bottle. The extra pressure forces extra water into the cap so that it sinks.

Note: Before starting this experiment, block the airhole on the pen cap. Don't forget to unplug it again when you have finished.

3 Cut the rubber in a circle about 1¼ in (3 cm) wider than the jar top. Stretch it over the top of the jar and tie it around the neck with the string.

Press the rubber down into the neck of the jar. Watch what happens to the pen cap. It should slowly sink. Release your fingers and it should float up again.

HOW TO MAKE A SIPHON

You will need

✔ A length of clean, flexible plastic tube about 2 to 3 ft (0.6 to 1 m) long.

✔ Two large plastic bottles

✔ A jug

1 Set up the bottles on a waterproof table, or outdoors. Then fill one bottle with water from the jug.

In the real world

IRRIGATION SYSTEMS

Growing crops need huge amounts of water. It takes around 20,000 pints (10,000 liters) of water to grow every 2 lbs (1 kg) of food. In dry countries, there is often not enough water for crops to thrive. Even in less arid countries, farmers may need more water to boost crop production. Many farmers channel water onto the land. This is called irrigation. In recent years, more and more farmland has been irrigated, especially in Asia. A fifth of the world's cropland is now irrigated, and this land produces over a third of the world's food.

2 Dip one end of the tube in the full bottle. Take a deep breath and suck the water through the tube to fill it.

The empty bottle drinks from the full bottle in a process called siphoning. The siphon works because the pressure of water in the full bottle is greater than it is in the empty bottle. The difference in pressure drives the water through the tube. The siphon will stop when the water in each bottle is at the same height and the pressure is equal.

3 Lift the bottle above shoulder height. Stop sucking and clamp your thumb over the end of the tube.

Place the end of the tube in the empty bottle, taking your thumb away as you do. You will see at once that the empty water bottle starts drinking water from the full bottle.

In focus

PUMPS

Siphons only work when there is a difference in water pressure, which means they only work "downhill." To lift water up, you need a pump. The simplest pumps are old-fashioned hand pumps, which date back to at least 300 B.C. They lift a little water at a time from underground with a plunger or piston moved up and down by a hand lever. Modern motorized pumps use rotating gears or vanes to move the water.

FLOATING AND SINKING

Some things, such as corks, float on water, while others, such as stones, sink. Objects that float are lighter or less dense than water. Things that sink are heavier or more dense.

Whenever an object is put in water, its weight pushes downward. As the object pushes down, it pushes water out of the way. The water pushes the object back with a force equal to

The air inside this rubber ring is less dense than water so the ring floats.

Did you know?

You can lift someone quite heavy when you are standing in a swimming pool, because the upthrust of the water makes the person more buoyant.

Our scientific understanding of why things float and why things sink dates back to the brilliant Ancient Greek thinker Archimedes. Archimedes (c.287–212 B.C.) lived in Syracuse in Sicily. He made many important contributions to science, including the theory of levers, and devised many ingenious inventions. It was Archimedes who realized that when an object is immersed in water, its weight pushes down, but the water pushes it back up with a force equal to the weight of water displaced. This is called Archimedes' Principle.

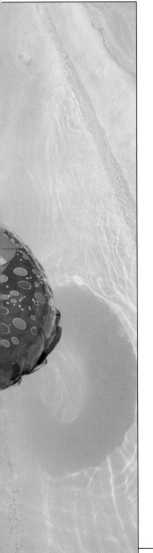

the weight of water displaced (pushed out of the way). This pushing back is called "upthrust." Upthrust makes things lighter in water than they are in air. The loss of weight is called buoyancy.

If the object is less dense than water, the weight of water displaced is greater than the weight of the object. The upthrust pushes the object and makes it float. If the object is more dense than water, the weight of water displaced is less than the weight of the object. The upthrust is too small to keep the object afloat.

Corks float because they are much less dense than water. Steel ships float because although steel is denser than water, the ships' hulls are full of air. They sink until enough water is displaced to match the weight of air in the hull.

FISH AND THEIR SWIMBLADDERS

To keep them afloat, many fish have a special air bag inside their bodies called a swimbladder. Without this, the fish would have to swim all the time to avoid sinking. Sharks and rays have no swimbladder, and they drift slowly to the bottom whenever they stop swimming.

Just as air in a buoyancy ring keeps you afloat in the swimming pool, the gas in a fish's swimbladder helps it float at a particular depth in the sea. As a fish dives deeper, the water pressure increases. The extra water pressure squeezes the gas in the bladder. To avoid sinking the fish inflates the bladder with extra gas made in its blood. When the fish swims higher, the water pressure decreases and the extra gas is let out.

FLOATERS AND SINKERS

You will need

✓ Household objects for testing. Choose materials that will not be damaged by water

✓ Wooden and metal spoons

✓ Various fruits and vegetables including oranges

✓ Gravel and pumice stone

1 Fill a basin with water. Test if similar things like spoons always float, or does the material they are made of matter?

What is happening?

The main thing this experiment shows is that some materials sink and others float. If you lift the materials that float, such as wood, you will find that they all feel lighter than those that sink. They float because they are less dense than the water. Materials like metal and stone usually feel heavy and sink because they are more dense. The pumice stone is an exception because it contains so many air bubbles that it is less dense than water, so floats. The orange floats because the peel contains air bubbles, but when it is peeled the air is lost and the orange sinks.

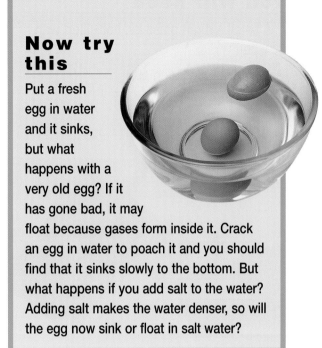

Now try this

Put a fresh egg in water and it sinks, but what happens with a very old egg? If it has gone bad, it may float because gases form inside it. Crack an egg in water to poach it and you should find that it sinks slowly to the bottom. But what happens if you add salt to the water? Adding salt makes the water denser, so will the egg now sink or float in salt water?

2 Do the same things always float? Or can altering them make them sink? What happens if you peel an orange?

Test all your objects and you will find some things float and others sink. You may also find that some things, such as a washcloth, float when dry then sink when they become full of water. Other things that float at first, like the orange, will sink when they are altered in some way. See if you can alter any sinking things to make them float. Make one list of those that sink and another of those that float. Then see if you can work out what the things that float all have in common.

DISPLACEMENT

You will need

✓ A small airtight glass jar, half-filled with water

✓ A plastic measuring cup

✓ Paper and pen

✓ A kitchen scale

✓ A larger jar

1 Stand the large jar in the pan of the kitchen scale. Fill it exactly to the brim with water, taking care not to spill any water into the scale pan. Note the weight.

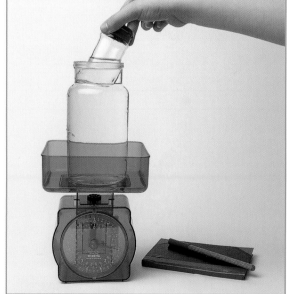

2 Gently lower the small jar into the large jar. This will make some water spill out into the scales pan. Note the weight now. The weight has increased.

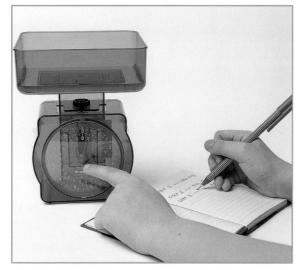

What is happening?

This experiment shows how the weight of water displaced—and so the upthrust—is exactly equal to the weight of the object. You will also find that subtracting either the weight of the water displaced or the weight of the jar from the combined weight in step 2 will give you the original weight that you had in step 1.

3 Take the large jar out of the pan. Note the weight of water spilled into the pan. This is the water that was displaced by the small jar.

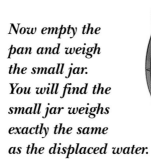

Now empty the pan and weigh the small jar. You will find the small jar weighs exactly the same as the displaced water.

FLOATING STEADILY

You will need

- ✓ Two plastic soft drinks bottles with screwable caps
- ✓ Plasticine or re-usable poster putty
- ✓ Scissors
- ✓ Basin or tank of water

1 Cut the bottle in half, stick a blob of putty on the rim, and try to float it. Since it is top-heavy, it falls over and may sink.

In the real world

For serious canoeists, there is nothing to match the thrill of riding a canoe through rough, white water on a mountain stream—but they must have a good roll technique to right the canoe should it tip over.

CANOE ROLL

Canoes are very light, with much of the weight quite high up. Often used in rough waters, they frequently tip over. Once over, the canoeist's weight pulls him down so that he hangs upside down underwater. The first lesson many canoeists learn is how to right the boat. There are various techniques, but the aim is always for the canoeist to shift his weight so that it pulls him back up, like the weighted bottle in the experiment. In a simple "roll," the canoeist shifts his upper body and one knee, so his weight pulls the boat back, while he uses his paddle to push up his body.

2 Stick the blob of putty on the base of the bottle half. It should now float upright quite stably.

Stick a ridge of putty down one side of the uncut bottle and screw the cap on. Now, no matter how you try to sink or capsize it, it always rights itself.

What is happening?

Boats need to be stable to stay afloat. With the weight at the top of an open boat (the half bottle), it can easily capsize, flood with water, and sink. Adding weight to the bottom makes a boat less likely to capsize and sink. The weight can be added on the outside as a keel, or the inside as a ballast of sand—here, the putty on the bottle. This is how most big ships work. Additional fins on the hull stabilize it still further. Many rescue lifeboats combine the weight in the bottom with a watertight hull to make a self-righting, virtually unsinkable boat, as in the uncut bottle-boat.

HEAVY WATER

Just as solids that are less dense than water float, so too do liquids that are less dense—so long as they do not mix. You can often see thin layers of oil shimmering on the surface of puddles in the road. The oil is dropped by trucks and automobiles. It is less dense than water so it floats on rainwater. Liquids that are more dense than water sink.

In the same way, cold water sinks in warm water because cold water is more dense. Warm water floats up in cold water because it is less dense. This can create convection currents. Convection is when warm water is "conveyed," or carried

Bubbles of olive oil float on water because the oil is lighter than the water.

Did you know?

Nuclear power plants use a special kind of water called "heavy water." Ordinary water molecules are made from oxygen and ordinary hydrogen. Heavy water molecules are made from a special "heavy" kind of hydrogen called deuterium. Heavy water is slightly denser than ordinary water but otherwise much the same. It is very effective at containing nuclear reactions.

upward, in cold water while cold water sinks in another place.

The upward movement of warm water and the downward movement of cold water combine to create a circulation. This circulation is a convection current. You can see small convection currents in water boiling in a saucepan on an electric burner. Convection currents on a much larger scale play an important part in the oceans and in the structure of the earth.

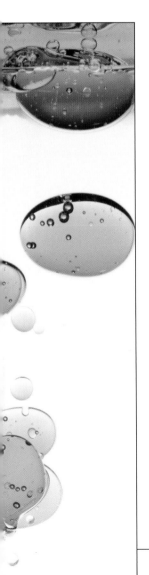

In focus

HOW THE WORLD'S DEEP OCEAN CURRENTS WORK

The surface waters of the oceans are circulating round and round all the time because they are blown along by the wind. But the whole ocean is circulating very slowly too, not just the surface water. Slow, deep circulation is driven by differences in the density of seawater. These circulations are called "thermohaline" circulations because the differences in density are created by the temperature and salt content of the water. ("Thermo" means temperature and "haline" means salt.) Cold water is more dense than warm water. Saltier water is more dense than water with a lower concentration of salt. Small changes in density can make large changes in the circulation.

One important thermohaline circulation happens because dense water forms in the polar regions where the air is very cold. Salt is left behind as seawater freezes into ice, making the water here extra dense. Dense water develops like this beneath the Arctic and Antarctic ice sheets, then sinks deep down and spreads slowly out toward the equator.

Surface ocean currents rotate clockwise in the Northern Hemisphere and counterclockwise in the Southern Hemisphere.

FLOATING LIQUIDS

You will need

- ✔ Rubbing alcohol
- ✔ Assorted food colors
- ✔ Cooking oil
- ✔ A tall glass
- ✔ A pitcher
- ✔ Water

1 Add a few drops of food color to water and pour the water into a straight-sided glass to about a quarter full.

In focus

DEEP OCEAN CURRENTS

The surface of the ocean is always on the move, blown by the wind. The whole ocean is on the move very slowly, too, driven by differences in the density of seawater. These differences are partly created by temperature—cold water is denser than warm—and partly by the amount of salt. Typically, dense water forms in Polar regions where it is cold and weighed down by salt left behind when the sea freezes to make sea ice. This dense polar water sinks and spreads deep down, outward towards the Equator. Warmer water floats back over the top toward the Polar regions.

Warm water spreads from the Equator near the surface

Arctic ice

Antarctic ice

Cold, dense water sinks and moves towards the Equator deep down

Once the oil has settled into a clear layer, add food color to the rubbing alcohol. Tilt the glass gently, as before, and pour the alcohol down the side of the glass so that it flows across the top of the oil. Take care not to pour so fast that the alcohol breaks through the oil. Stand the glass upright.

2 Tilt the glass and slowly pour the oil so that it flows over the water without mixing. If it mixes, leave it to stand.

Rubbing alcohol

Oil

Water

What is happening?

Just like solids, liquids that are less dense than water float, providing they do not mix. Oil is less dense than water. It does not mix with water, so it floats in a layer on top of the water. This is why you can often see multi-colored patches of oil dropped by vehicles floating on puddles on the road. Rubbing alcohol is less dense than either oil or water, so it floats on oil. However, rubbing alcohol mixes easily with water, so if it was not for the layer of oil, it would mix in with the water and so become indistinguishable from it.

HOW TO MAKE A HYDROMETER

You will need

- ✔ Re-usable poster putty
- ✔ Identical drinking glasses
- ✔ Plastic drinking straws (check that they float evenly)
- ✔ Cooking oil
- ✔ Marker pen
- ✔ Water
- ✔ Salt

1 Cut each straw in half and make marks across each one at regular intervals. Stick some poster putty on one end of each straw. This is your hydrometer.

In the real world

THE PLIMSOLL LINE

Ships float at different heights if the density of water varies. They float higher in seawater than in freshwater because the salt in seawater makes it dense. They also float higher in dense, cold seas than in warm seas. The higher the ship floats, the more weight it can safely carry. Some ships are marked with lines to show the level to which they can be loaded. There are different lines for tropical water, freshwater, summer, and winter. Some of these lines are called Plimsoll lines after their inventor, English politician Samuel Plimsoll.

2 Pour some water into one glass. Lower a hydrometer, weighted-end first, into the water and let it float upright. Note which mark the water comes to.

3 Fill the second glass with exactly the same amount of water. Add a tablespoon of salt and stir well. Take another reading with a hydrometer.

Fill the third glass with cooking oil and lower a hydrometer into it. Note where the water comes to.

What is happening?

The hydrometer shows how dense a liquid is because it sinks deep into a light liquid like oil and less deep in a heavier one like salt water. Typically, the scale on a hydrometer is set from the height at which the instrument floats in pure water. The densities of other liquids are called "relative densities."

SURFACE TENSION

Bubbles are round because their outside layer is pulled inward by surface tension.

Drops of water are always round. Look at the condensation on a soda can or raindrops hitting a window. They are round because of surface tension.

Surface tension happens because water molecules attract each other. In the middle of a drop, there are lots of molecules pulling toward each other in all directions. At the surface, molecules are only pulled back into the water, because there are no molecules pulling the other way. So the

water pulls its surface tight around it, like a stretchy skin.

Surface tension is quite weak and only pulls small droplets into balls. But it has many effects. It is surface tension that makes the water surface form an arc called a "meniscus" when you fill a glass right to the brim.

Surface tension allows small insects, such as pond skaters, to walk on water. It is also surface tension that keeps water from getting through the tiny holes in fabrics such as cotton. This is why tents keep out rain as long as you do not bang the fabric and break the surface tension.

In focus

HOW SOAP WORKS

Water on its own is not much good at cleaning. To remove grease and grime you need to add soap or detergent to the water.

Soaps and detergents clean because their molecules are attracted to both water and grease. One end of the molecule is hydrophilic (meaning water-loving) and is attracted to water. The other end is hydrophobic (water-hating); it likes grease and dirt. The hydrophobic end of the molecule digs its way into the dirt. The hydrophilic end is drawn into the water, and this pulls the dirt away.

Grease often will not wash off surfaces because surface tension in water stops the water from getting into the grease. Detergents often contain special molecules called surfactants. These lower the surface tension, which increases the water's ability to make things wet.

Soaps are made by boiling animal fat or vegetable oil with sodium hydroxide. Scents and colors are added to make the soap more attractive to use.

MAKING A POWERED BOAT

You will need

- ✔ A large bowl of water
- ✔ A matchstick
- ✔ Detergent
- ✔ Scissors
- ✔ Foil

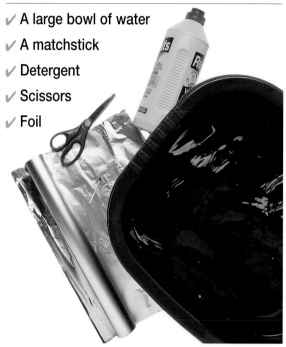

1 Flatten a piece of foil about 2 in (5 cm) square. Squeeze the foil between two books to make sure it is quite flat.

2 Cut a boatlike shape from the foil, with a small notch in the middle of the "stern." Smooth out the boat again.

3 Fill the bowl with water, and lower the boat gently onto the surface. Surface tension will keep your foil boat floating.

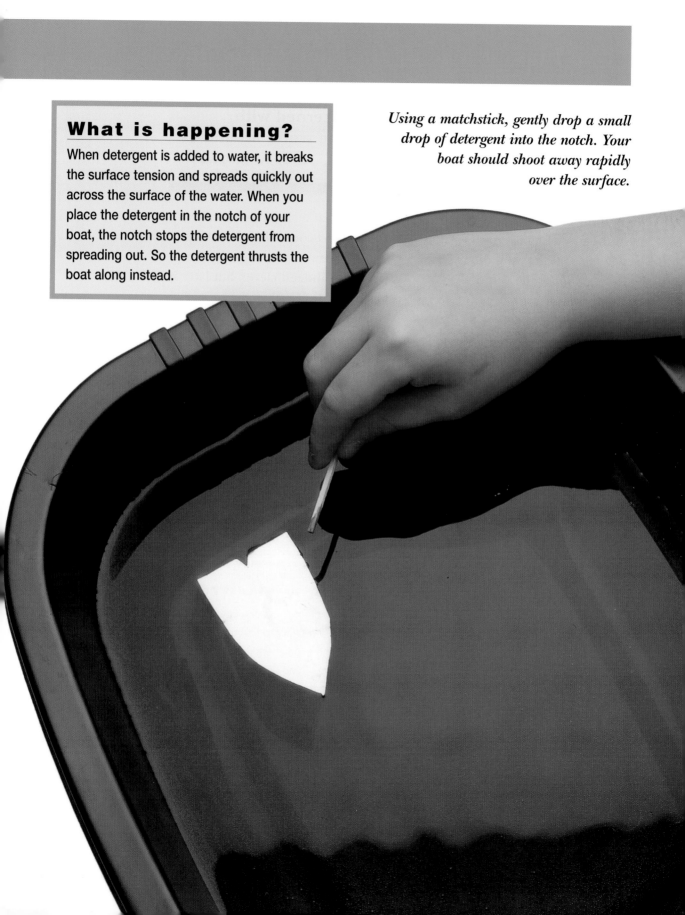

What is happening?

When detergent is added to water, it breaks the surface tension and spreads quickly out across the surface of the water. When you place the detergent in the notch of your boat, the notch stops the detergent from spreading out. So the detergent thrusts the boat along instead.

Using a matchstick, gently drop a small drop of detergent into the notch. Your boat should shoot away rapidly over the surface.

The Importance of Science Experiments

Science is about knowledge: it is concerned with knowing and trying to understand the world around us. The word comes from the Latin word, *scire*, to know.

In the early seventeenth century, the great English thinker Francis Bacon suggested that the best way to learn about the world was not simply to think about it, but to go out and look for yourself—to make observations and try things out. Ever since then, scientists have tried to approach their work with a mixture of observation and experiment. Scientists insist that an idea or theory must be tested by observation and experiment before it is widely accepted.

All the experiments in this book have been tried before, and the theories behind them are widely accepted. But that it is no reason why you should accept them. Once you have done all the experiments in this book, you will know the ideas are true not because we have told you so, but because you have seen for yourself.

All too often in science there is an external factor interfering with the result which the scientist just has not thought of. Sometimes this can make the experiment seem to work when it has not, as well as making it fail. One scientist conducted a lot of demonstrations to show that a clever horse called Hans could count things and tap out the answer with his hoof. The horse was indeed clever, but later it was found that rather than counting, he was getting clues from tiny unconscious movements of the scientist's eyebrows.

This is why it is very important when conducting experiments to be as careful as you possibly can. The more casual you are, the more "eyebrow factors" you will let in. There will always be some things that you cannot control. But the more precise you are, the less these are likely to affect the outcome.

What went wrong?

However careful you are, your experiments may not work. If so, you should try to find out where you went wrong. Then repeat the experiment until you are absolutely sure you are doing everything right. Scientists learn as much, if not more, from experiments that go wrong as those that succeed. In 1929, Alexander Fleming discovered the first antibiotic drug, penicillin, when he noticed that a bacteria culture he was growing for an experiment had gone moldy—and that the mold seemed to kill the bacteria. A poor scientist would probably have thrown the moldy culture away. A good scientist is one who looks for alternative explanations for unexpected results.

Glossary

acid: A compound that dissolves in water to produce hydrogen ions. Dilute acids taste sour. Strong acids are corrosive.

alkali: A base that will dissolve in water, such as ammonia and the hydroxides of sodium calcium, and potassium.

alloy: A combination of metals and other elements that is often stronger than a metal in its pure form.

atom: The smallest part of any chemical element. Anything smaller is no longer a chemical element. Each element has its own unique atom.

ballast: Extra weight put in the bottom of a ship to weigh it down and make it more stable. This may be extra cargo, or simply stones, gravel, or sand.

base: The chemical opposite of an acid; a substance that neutralizes an acid by accepting hydrogen ions.

boiling point: The temperature at which a liquid turns into a gas. At normal atmospheric pressure pure water boils at 212 °F (100 °C).

bond: A link holding atoms together to make molecules.

buoyancy: The ability of an object to float.

charge: A quantity of electricity.

chromatography: A method of separating out the components of a mixture.

compound: A combination of two or more elements, joined chemically by bonds between atoms. Compounds have a double chemical name like sodium chloride.

condensation: The change from a gas to a liquid. As a gas cools down, its particles move slower and eventually clump together. The gas then forms drops of liquid.

convection: The floating up of warm water in one place and sinking of cold water in another, often resulting in currents.

covalent bond: A chemical bond in which electrons are shared between atoms.

density: The amount of a substance (mass) in a certain volume; a measure of how tightly packed the material is.

displaced: Pushed out of the way.

electron: The very tiny particles that circle the nucleus of an atom. They are negatively charged.

elements: The very simplest chemical substances, each with a one word chemical name. There are about 117 of them. They cannot be split into simper substances by chemical reactions.

equation: A way of writing down the chemicals involved in a reaction, showing the chemicals before and those after.

evaporation: The change from liquid to gas. When a liquid warms up, some particles move fast enough to escape from its surface and turn into gas.

formula: The symbol for a molecule of an element or

compound, showing the number of atoms involved.

freezing point: Temperature at which a liquid turns into a solid. Pure water freezes at 32 °F (0 °C) at normal atmospheric pressure.

front: Dividing line between two different air masses.

humidity: Amount of moisture in the air.

hydroelectric power: Electricity that is made by the force of water power.

hydrogen bond: Special bonds that hold water molecules together. They are caused by an attraction between the oxygen ions in one water molecule and the hydrogen ions in another water molecule.

hydrology: A branch of science dealing with the circulation of water over the earth and in the atmosphere.

hygrometer: Instrument for measuring humidity.

ion: An atom or molecule that has lost or gained an electron. An ion has a positive or a negative electrical charge, while an atom is neutral.

ionic bond: A bond between two or more ions, created as one atom donates an electron to another atom and becomes negatively charged. They are joined by mutual electrical attraction.

irrigation: To supply cropland with extra water; it is mainly used in hot, dry countries.

magma: The hot molten rock that wells up beneath Earth's crust from the interior. Magma is called lava when it emerges on the Earth's surface.

melting point: The temperature at which a solid turns liquid as it warms up. The melting point of ice is 32 °F (0 °C).

meniscus: The curved upper surface of a liquid where it touches the edge of a container.

mixture: A combination of substances in which there are no bonds between chemicals, so they can be separated physically.

molecule: The smallest bit of a substance that can exist by itself. It is made up of one or more atoms. Each molecule of a substance has an identical combination of

atoms. Water molecules are made from three atoms: one oxygen and two hydrogen.

neutron: One of two kinds of particle in the nucleus of an atom. It carries no electrical charge and is therefore neutral.

nucleus: The central cluster of protons and neutrons in an atom.

oxidation: A reaction such as rusting or burning in which a chemical gains oxygen or loses hydrogen, or an atom or ion loses electrons.

polar molecule: Molecules with slightly negative parts and slightly positive parts. Water is an example of a polar molecule.

precipitation: The falling of water from clouds as rain, snow, sleet, or hail.

proton: One of two kinds of particle in the nucleus of an atom. It carries a positive electrical charge that balances the negative charge of an electron.

reaction: When chemicals meet and change each other to form new chemicals.

relative density: The density of a substance in relation to the density of pure water.

salinity: A measure of how much salt is dissolved in a volume of water.

solute: The part of a solution that has dissolved in the liquid.

solvent: A liquid able to dissolve substances.

surface tension: The force that forms across the surface of a body of water because of the attractions between water molecules.

surfactants: Special molecules that affect the surface tension of water.

suspension: A liquid in which fine specks of solid are mixed but are not dissolved.

swimbladder: An air-filled sac inside the body of many types of fish. By filling the sac with air, or by squeezing air out of it, fish can control their buoyancy.

upthrust: The force that pushes up against an object when the object is placed in a fluid such as water. An object floats if its weight is the same as the upthrust. It sinks if the upthrust cannot support its weight.

viscosity: A liquid's resistance to flow, or stickiness.

water vapor: Water in its invisible gaseous state, formed when liquid water evaporates completely.

Index

Page numbers in **bold** indicate photos or illustrations.